FOUNDATIONS

of Restaurant Management & Culinary Arts

Level One

Activity Guide

National Restaurant Association

Prentice Hall

Boston Columbus Indianapolis New York San Francisco Upper Saddle River Amsterdam
Cape Town Dubai London Madrid Milan Munich Paris Montreal Toronto
Delhi Mexico City Sao Paulo Sydney Hong Kong Seoul Singapore Taipei Tokyo

Editorial Director: Vernon Anthony
Executive Editor: Wendy Craven
Editorial Assistant: Lenore Chait
Director of Marketing: David Gesell
Campaign Marketing Manager: Leigh Ann Sims
School Marketing Manager: Laura Cutone
Senior Marketing Assistant: Les Roberts
Associate Managing Editor: Alexandrina Benedicto Wolf
Project Manager: Kris Roach
Senior Operations Supervisor: Pat Tonneman
Operations Specialist: Deidra Skahill

Cover Designer: Jane Diane Ricciardi
Manager, Rights and Permissions: Zina Arabia
Cover Art: Kipling Swehla
NRAS Product Management Team: Janet Benoit, Megan Meyer, William Nolan, Rachel Peña, and Wendi Safstrom
Product Development and Project Management: Emergent Learning, LLC
Writing and Text Development: Mary Nunaley
Composition: Phil Velikan
Printer/Binder: Edwards Brothers
Cover Printer: Phoenix Color

Prentice Hall
an imprint of

PearsonSchool.com/careertech

ISBN 10: 0-13-707050-0
ISBN 13: 978-0-13-707050-3

Preface

This Activity Guide accompanies *Foundations of Restaurant Management & Culinary Arts—Level One*. It is designed to reinforce what you're learning in your textbook. You will find many different types of activities per chapter. To use the Activity Guide most effectively:

- Follow the directions. If you are instructed to research a topic on the Internet or in your textbook before completing the activity, be certain to gather all the information you need before you answer.

- Use your text to help you complete the activities.

- Check your answers for accuracy. If you have difficulty with answers, return to the text and read the information again.

- It is very difficult to "play catch-up." Complete the activities when they are assigned.

Note to the teacher: The answer key to the workbook is included on the Teacher's Resource DVD-ROM. However, many of the activities in the workbook don't have "correct" answers, so student responses will vary.

Table of Contents

Chapter 4

Chapter 5

Chapter 6

Chapter 7

Chapter 11

Chapter 12

Chapter 1

Activity 1.1
Test Your Knowledge of the Restaurant and Foodservice Industry IQ

Directions

Mark each of the following statements related to the restaurant and foodservice industry as either true (T) or false (F). For each answer that is false, rewrite it to make it true.

Part 1—Overview of the Foodservice Industry

_____ 1. The foodservice industry has average annual sales of over $500 million.

_____

_____

_____ 2. There are more than 945,000 restaurant and foodservice operations in the United States today.

_____

_____

_____ 3. The restaurant and foodservice industry employs more than 20 million people in the United States.

_____

_____

_____ 4. Over 50 percent of restaurant and foodservice managers are women.

_____

_____

_____ 5. The industry is expected to continue growing over the next decade.

_____

_____

_____ 6. With focus and hard work, it is possible to build a rewarding and long-lasting career.

_____

_____

_____ 7. Approximately 10 percent of eating and drinking establishments in the United States are owned by women.

_____

_____

_____ 8. If you like food, people, celebrating, or just going out, the restaurant and foodservice industry offers many exciting opportunities.

_____

_____

Part 2—The Restaurant and Foodservice Industry

_____ 1. Most people eat at restaurant and foodservice operations for enjoyment and entertainment, which would make the restaurant and foodservice industry a knowledge industry.

_____

_____

_____ 2. The industry can be divided into two major segments: commercial and noncommercial.

_____

_____

_____ 3. The commercial segment includes restaurants, catering, stadiums, and cruise ships.

_____

_____

_____ 4. In quick-service restaurants, guests place their orders with a server who then delivers it to the table and receives payment after the meal is finished.

_____

_____

_____ 5. Retail stores offer prepared meals that can be eaten in the store or taken home.

_____

_____

_____ 6. Food on most cruise ships is available only during set dining hours.

_____

_____

_____ 7. Schools and health-care facilities are two types of noncommercial foodservice operations.

_____

_____

_____ 8. In the noncommercial foodservice segment, either contract feeding or self-operators handle foodservice.

_____

_____

Part 3—The Hospitality Industry

_____ 1. Travel and tourism is defined as the combination of all the services that people need and are willing to pay for when they are away from home.

_____

_____

_____ 2. Hospitality refers to the services people use and receive when they are away from home.

_____

_____

_____ 3. The U.S. travel and tourism industry averages sales of over $500 billion a year.

_____

_____

_____ 4. Tourism is travel for business purposes.

_____

_____

_____ 5. In addition to foodservice, lodging and event management are important segments of the hospitality industry.

_____

_____

_____ 6. Event management includes stadiums, expositions, and retail establishments.

_____

_____

_____ 7. The lodging sector includes hotels, motels, and resorts.

_____

_____

_____ 8. In the 1920s, travelers began to journey by air.

_____

_____

Activity 1.2
Crossword Puzzle—History of Foodservice

Directions

Complete the following statements and then use the answers to complete the crossword puzzle.

Across

3. _____ _____ was a system of production were workers worked from home to produce goods.

4. An association comprised of people with similar interests or professions is a _____.

6. A resting place on a stagecoach route where travelers could get a meal and a bed for a night was called a _____ _____.

7. The process of making milk safe to drink is called _____.

10. One of two cooking guilds that established many of the cooking and professional standards still used today is called the _____ _____ _____.

11. The first building in the United States to open as a hotel opened in New York City in 1794 and was called the _____ _____.

13. The sole purpose of a medieval dinner was to _____.

15. The time between the end of the Roman Empire and the start of the Renaissance is known as the _____ _____.

16. The original term for a restaurant was _____.

19. _____ _____ was an ancient Roman gourmet who is said to have written one of the earliest cookbooks.

20. The first quick-service restaurant, _____ _____, opened in 1921.

21. _____ _____ is known as the father of canning, because he invented a way to can food and keep it safe and fresh.

22. _____ _____ _____ allows those who want to eat at home without cooking an option.

Down

1. An early explorer who introduced spices such as curry and cardamon to Europe was _____ _____.

2. An elaborate and refined system of food preparation is known as _____ _____.

5. Private clubs visited by ancient Greeks were called _____.

8. _____ was the home of the first coffee house, which opened in 1650.

9. _____ _____ _____ introduced the French to the fork and use of silverware during the Renaissance.

10. An assembly line process developed after the Gold Rush to quickly and cheaply serve food to a large number of diners is a _____.

12. The scientific revolution that came after the Renaissance was known as the _____.

14. The time in history that demonstrated a renewed interest in all things Greek and Roman was the

    _____.

17. Establishments in ancient Greece that catered to travelers, traders, and diplomats were called _____.

18. A lodging operation typically found along highways and offers a place to sleep, bathe, and eat is a

    _____.

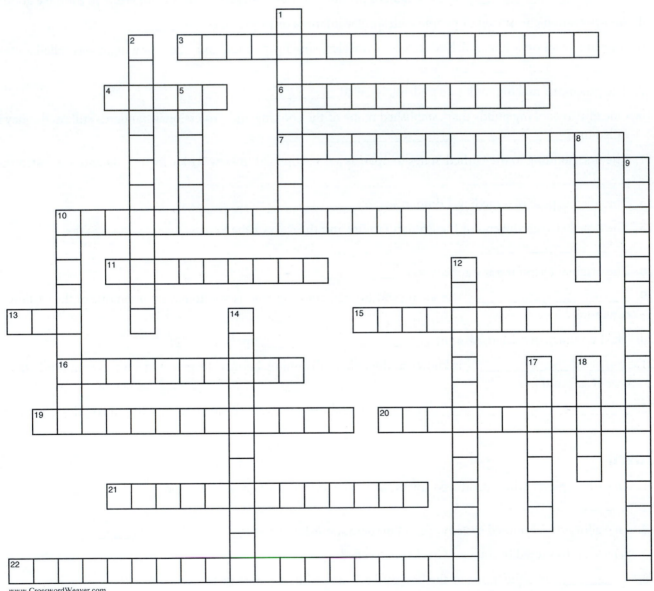

www.CrosswordWeaver.com

Activity 1.3
Report/Presentation—Famous Chefs/Entrepreneurs

Directions
Select a chef from the list brainstormed by the class.

Include answers to the following questions in your report:

1. Where was this person born?
2. Why did he or she decide to become a chef or entrepreneur?
3. How did he or she train for his or her profession (apprenticeship, culinary school, other)?
4. What contributions has he or she made to the hospitality and/or foodservice field?
5. What dish or business is he or she most famous for?
6. List three interesting facts about this person that you did not know.

Take your notes below. Present your findings to the class.

_____

_____

_____

_____

_____

_____

_____

_____

_____

_____

_____

_____

_____

_____

_____

_____

Activity 1.4
Menu Design—Banquets through History

Directions

Research the following periods in time and create a sample banquet menu for each time period.

- Ancient Greece or Ancient Rome

- Medieval times (Middle Ages)

- Renaissance

- Twentieth century

Use the space below to take your notes. Attach your menus to this sheet.

Activity 1.5
Fill in the Blank—Contributions of Entrepreneurs to the Foodservice and Hospitality Industry

Directions

Fill in the blanks using the information you learned in Section 1.2, "The History of Hospitality and Foodservice."

1. In 1837, the _____ opened a group of restaurants in Manhattan, beginning the first restaurant chain.

2. The Harvey House Restaurant opened in _____ to serve the needs of travelers on the transcontinental railroad, becoming one of the most popular restaurants of the time.

3. Roy Allen and Frank Wright sold the rights to allow people to sell their root beer. This action created the first _____.

4. _____ partnered with the McDonald's brothers to franchise their hamburger operation. By 1963 there were over 500 McDonald's locations in the United States.

5. Norman Brinker opened the first _____ restaurant, a full-service restaurant to serve middle class customers.

6. The _____ group operates Red Lobster, Olive Garden, and Bahama Breeze restaurants.

7. The first _____ opened in Seattle, Washington, in 1971. Starbucks currently has more than 16,000 stores worldwide.

8. _____ founded the Lettuce Entertain You Enterprises in the early 1970s.

9. One of the first national fine dining chains is _____, which was founded by Ruth Fertel in the late 1970s.

10. The first _____ restaurant opened in 1921 in Wichita, Kansas.

Activity 1.6
Types of Establishments
Providing Foodservice

Directions

Match the description of the type of establishment to the correct category.

_____ Health Services   _____ Conventions   _____ Lodging

_____ Catering   _____ Retail/Shopping

_____ Military   _____ Theme Park

1. A place offering exhibits, rides, entertainment, and other attractions, often with a theme connecting everything.

2. Provides foodservice ranging from a light breakfast to gourmet meals for overnight guests that stay at a property.

3. Provides foodservice for everything ranging from special events to large events including golf tournaments, weddings, and dinners.

4. Serving over 1 million meals a year at locations all over the world.

5. Provides food options to tourists who choose shopping as a recreational activity.

6. An aspect of the industry expected to grow as baby boomers age, includes hospitals, long-term care facilities and assisted living.

7. A gathering of people who have something in common and meet annually.

Activity 1.7
Job Information Interview

Directions

Select a person whose job you are curious about and set up an informational interview with him or her. You will need about 30 minutes for the interview. Prepare several information-gathering questions to ask that person. Be prepared to discuss in class what you discovered about this job.

Sample Questions

1. What are some of your job responsibilities?
2. Briefly describe your typical workday.
3. What are the most interesting and least interesting parts of your job?
4. What made you choose this type of work?
5. What type of training and schooling is required for your job?
6. What were the jobs that led you to the job you have now?
7. What types of entry-level jobs are available in this field?
8. What are the various salary ranges in this field?
9. What are the basic qualifications for someone in this field?
10. What is the best way to obtain a position and start a career in this field?
11. In general, how do you like working in this industry?

Use the space below to take your notes. Attach additional pages as necessary. Present your findings to the class.

_____

_____

_____

_____

_____

_____

_____

_____

_____

_____

_____

_____

_____

Activity 1.8
Research—Career Pathways

Directions

Select a possible career path for yourself from one of the careers suggested in your book or a related field in hospitality or foodservice that interests you. Include answers to the following questions in your report. After completing your report, share the results with your partner and compare career options.

1. How much training or formal education is required for this position?

2. What are the opportunities for growth and advancement in this position within the next five years?

3. What is the starting salary for an entry-level position in this career area?

4. What is the salary for an experienced person in this career area?

5. In addition to formal education or training, what skills are required to be successful in this career?

6. What are three drawbacks to working in this career area?

7. What are three benefits to working in this career area?

8. Where can you find more information about this career path?

Use the space below to take your notes. Attach additional pages as necessary. Present your findings to the class.

_____

_____

_____

_____

_____

_____

_____

_____

_____

_____

_____

_____

_____

_____

_____

Activity 1.9
Writing a News Article

Create an article that could be used in the student newspaper, local newspaper, or a Web site that highlights a career in the foodservice industry. Use the interview from Activity 1.7–Job Information Interview as your guide.

When writing the news article, keep the following points in mind:

- Using the information from the interview, you will want to include answers to the questions: Who? What? Where? When? Why? How?

- Example:
  - Who: Chef John Baker
  - What: being a chef
  - When: after high school until today
  - Why: encourage students to enter the culinary field
  - How: by taking classes, working in the business

When you can answer these six questions, you are ready to write your article. Begin the process by adding details to the story. Use the information from the interview and also do some extra research using your textbook, the Internet, and other experts.

After you have written the general story, go back and write the opening paragraph or "lead." This is the first thing readers will see and should get them interested in reading the story.

Next step: Write the headline. This should be short and use action words to capture the reader's attention.

Last step: Revise your work:

- Ask someone to review the article for you.
- Check for spelling, grammar, and accuracy of information.

Use the space below to take your notes. Attach additional pages as necessary.

_____

_____

_____

_____

_____

_____

_____

_____

_____

_____

Activity 1.10
Create a Marketing Flyer for a Hotel

Directions

You have been selected as an intern for a new hotel that just opened in town. One of your first tasks is to create a flyer that will be put into every guest room telling guests about the amenities the hotel has to offer them.

On the flyer include the following information:

- Welcome to the hotel
- 200 guest rooms
- Deluxe complimentary continental breakfast
- Includes: fresh fruit, pastries, made-to-order waffles, made-to-order omelets, juice, and hot beverages
- Indoor swimming pool
- Complimentary Wi-Fi
- In-room movies

The flyer will be used to give hotel guests more information about the property. Use the space below to draft the flyer. Attach the finished flyer to this sheet.

Chapter **2**

Activity 2.1
Test Your Food Safety IQ

Directions

Mark each of the following statements related to food safety as either true (T) or false (F). For each answer that is false, rewrite it to make it true.

_____ 1. Common foods such as beef, chicken, and fish can cause foodborne illnesses.

_____

_____

_____ 2. Even healthy people can cause illness by carrying microorganisms to food.

_____

_____

_____ 3. Proper handwashing includes scrubbing hands and arms for 10 to 15 seconds.

_____

_____

_____ 4. "Clean" and "sanitized" mean the same thing.

_____

_____

_____ 5. A turkey can be safely thawed at room temperature if it is left out no longer than 24 hours.

_____

_____

_____ 6. Receiving food during busy times is good because there are more people present.

_____

_____

_____ 7. Cooled food may be reheated in hot-holding equipment.

_____

_____

_____ 8. Even if your hands are clean, never touch any part of a glass, dish, or utensil that will touch food or a guest's mouth.

_____

_____

_____ 9. Washing dishes in detergent also sanitizes them.

_____

_____

_____ 10. Even water and ice can carry pathogens.

_____

_____

Activity 2.2
Create a Board Game—Foodborne Illness

Directions

Create a simple board game that will introduce the concepts of foodborne illness and sanitation to restaurant employees. Your game should include:

- A name for the game

- Game objective

- List of rules

- Drawing or photo of the game board

- Drawing or photo of tokens (playing pieces)

- Drawing or photo of game box (optional)

- Sample cards if using direction cards (think Monopoly)

Take your notes for your game in the space below. Attach additional pages as necessary. Present your game to the class.

_____

_____

_____

_____

_____

_____

_____

_____

_____

_____

_____

_____

_____

_____

_____

_____

_____

_____

_____

Activity 2.3
Fill in the Blank—FAT TOM

Directions

Fill in the blank with the correct information.

1. In order for pathogens to grow, they need a source of _____. This often includes carbohydrates or proteins such as beef or seafood.

2. Pathogens grow best in foods that have little or no acid. The levels of _____ are based on pH levels.

3. Pathogens grow best in the _____ danger zone (41°F to 135°F).

4. Food that has been in the temperature danger zone for an extended period of _____ may see a rapid increase in the growth of pathogens.

5. Humans need this to breathe and so do some pathogens. This element is _____.

6. Foods with large amounts of _____ can easily support the growth of pathogens.

7. The first letters of the words _____, _____, _____, _____, _____, and _____ create the phrase FAT TOM, which can help foodhandlers remember the conditions needed for pathogens to grow.

8. In most instances, a restaurant will only be able to control time and _____.

9. Food that is most vulnerable to pathogen growth may also be referred to as _____ because it needs time and temperature control.

10. _____ that can cause illness are called pathogens.

Activity 2.4
Public Service Announcement—Keeping Food Safe

Directions

Create a 30-second public service announcement about the potential of serving unsafe food. This 30-second alert should include what makes food unsafe, how to prevent making food unsafe, and where to learn more information.

Take your notes in the space below. Present your findings to the class.

_____

_____

_____

_____

_____

_____

_____

_____

_____

_____

_____

_____

_____

_____

_____

_____

_____

_____

_____

_____

_____

_____

_____

Activity 2.5
Fill in the Blank—Food Allergies

Directions

Complete the statements below.

1. A food allergy is the body's negative reaction to a food _____.

2. People with food allergies may become sick or _____ from eating even a small portion of an allergen.

3. When preparing food for customers, kitchen employees should be careful to avoid _____.

4. Many people suffer from nut allergies. The most common is an allergy to _____.

5. Tree nuts include nuts such as pecans and _____.

6. When answering customer questions about how food items are prepared, servers should be prepared to _____ alternative items.

7. Every year, nearly _____ people go to emergency rooms in the United States to be treated for severe allergies.

8. Signs of a food allergy reaction can include _____, itching, swelling of body parts, and even difficulty breathing.

9. _____ is a severe allergic reaction and is life threatening.

10. Many people with food allergies carry a device that allows them to give an injection of _____ and an antihistamine quickly in order to open up their airways.

Activity 2.6
Poster/Presentation—Food Safety First

Directions

You work for a national foodservice association that wants to publish a series of posters aimed at restaurant employees for National Food Safety Education Month®. Your team has been asked to choose a topic and create one of the posters. Each poster must convey information that is important for employees to know about specific food-safety topics and how they can keep food safe by following proper food safety practices.

You may choose from one of the following topics:

Microorganisms	Time
Bacteria	Temperature
Viruses	TCS foods
Parasites	Chemicals
Molds	Pests
Acidity	Moisture
Handwashing	Cross-contamination
Food allergens	FAT TOM

Part 1—Design a Poster

Working with your team, choose a food safety topic from the list above and design a food safety poster that meets the scenario requirements.

Refer to *Chapter 2: Keeping Food Safe* in your textbook for information related to the food safety topics listed above.

You may use the space provided on the next page to draw your final poster or as a practice space if you are creating your final poster with some other medium (poster board, computer, etc.).

Part 2—Develop and Deliver a Presentation

Design your presentation to address the following questions:

- What topic did your team choose?
- Why did your team choose this topic?
- How did your team research the topic?
- Why is this topic important for employees to understand?
- What is your team's poster trying to convey about this topic?

Take your notes in the space below. Present your findings to the class.

_____

_____

_____

_____

_____

_____

_____

_____

_____

_____

_____

_____

_____

_____

_____

_____

_____

_____

_____

_____

_____

Activity 2.7
A Case in Point—Donna's Morning

Directions

Read the case study below. As you read, think about what you have learned in this chapter about the importance of personal hygiene and health in keeping food safe. Then answer the questions at the end of the case study. Be prepared to share your answer.

Case Study

Donna is a kitchen employee in a high school cafeteria. It's 7:45 a.m. on Friday, and she has just woken up. She is scheduled to be at work and ready to go at 8:00 a.m. When she gets out of bed, her stomach feels queasy, but she ignores the feeling. Fortunately, Donna only lives a few minutes away from the school. She doesn't have time to take a shower and she is out of clean uniforms, so she wears the same uniform she wore on Thursday. Luck is not on Donna's side today. On her way to work, the "Check Engine" light comes on in her car, and she is forced to pull off the road and add oil to the engine.

When she walks through the cafeteria door, she realizes that she left her uniform hat at home. Her boss greets her gruffly and puts her to work right away making meatloaf. He instructs Donna to mix the raw hamburger with the seasoning and place it in pans to be baked. While preparing the meatloaf mixture, Donna's boss interrupts her and asks her to put the apple pie in the oven as soon as possible. Donna wipes her hands on her apron. She then takes the trays of apple pies out of the refrigerator and places them in the oven.

On her way back to preparing the meatloaf, Donna mentions to her boss that her stomach is bothering her. Her boss, thinking of how two of his employees already called in sick today, tells Donna to try to finish her shift. Donna agrees and heads to the restroom in hopes of relieving her symptoms. After quickly rinsing her hands in the restroom, she notices that there are no paper towels and wipes her hands on her apron. She then returns to the kitchen to continue preparing the meatloaf.

Case Study Questions

1. List at least three things Donna did wrong in regard to personal health and hygiene.

_____

_____

_____

2. What should Donna have done as soon as she got to work?

_____

_____

3. If you were Donna's manager, what would you have done when Donna told you she was sick?

_____

_____

Activity 2.8
Songwriting—The Importance of Handwashing

Directions

In order to avoid spreading diseases, you must wash hands properly. For this activity, work with a partner to write a song about proper handwashing techniques. Be sure to include why handwashing is important to preventing the spread of disease and the proper steps of handwashing.

The song can be based on a current song (melody) and should not be longer than 3 minutes.

Write your song in the space below. Present your song to the class.

_____

_____

_____

_____

_____

_____

_____

_____

_____

_____

_____

_____

_____

_____

_____

_____

_____

_____

_____

_____

_____

Activity 2.9
Crossword Puzzle—Food Safety

Directions

Complete the following statements and then use the answers to complete the crossword puzzle.

Across

1. Food served at an _____ _____ location has a greater risk of time-temperature abuse and contamination.

4. _____ stands for first-in, first-out and is a method used for rotating food in storage.

9. It is important to _____ thermometers regularly so they remain accurate.

11. _____ refers to food that needs time and temperature controls in order to remain safe.

12. A _____ stemmed thermometer is used to check temperatures of hot and cold food between 0°F and 220°F.

13 The _____ _____ _____ is the range of temperatures where pathogens grow most rapidly.

Down

2. The spread of pathogens from one surface or food to another is known as _____-_____.

3. The path that food takes within the foodservice operation is called the _____ __ _____.

5. Food deliveries should be inspected by trained staff and put away quickly as part of the _____ process.

6. The _____, or U.S. Department of Agriculture, proves that items meet the safety standards set by the government.

7. _____ is a frequency of radiation waves of the electromagnetic spectrum.

8. A device used to measure temperatures through the use of a metal probe and digital readout is called a _____.

10. Frozen food that will be cooked immediately can be thawed in a _____.

www.CrosswordWeaver.com

Activity 2.10
Food Safety Demonstration—How to Sanitize a Work Space

Directions

You have been asked by the local television station to demonstrate how to properly sanitize a surface in the kitchen. The producers are concerned that viewers are not aware that wiping down their cooking surfaces with just a paper towel is causing a minor outbreak of illness.

Part 1—Write a Script

Working as a team, create a script and practice what you will say to the audience. The presentation should not be more than 2 minutes. Be sure to demonstrate the steps for gathering equipment, working safely with cleaning supplies, and proper sanitizing practices.

Part 2—Demonstration

Do a demonstration of how to properly sanitize a surface. During the demonstration, explain how items can become cross–contaminated, why you should always wash your hands after handling raw products, and the difference between cleaning and sanitizing.

Take your notes in the space below. Present your demonstration to the class. If video equipment is available, record the demonstration.

_____

_____

_____

_____

_____

_____

_____

_____

_____

_____

_____

_____

_____

_____

Chapter **3**

Activity 3.1
Test Your Workplace Safety IQ

Directions

Mark each of the following statements related to workplace safety as either true (T) or false (F). For each answer that is false, rewrite it to make it true.

Part I—Safety and the Law

_____ 1. Liability is the legal responsibility that one person has to another.

_____

_____

_____ 2. Reasonable care is a legal term that means a judge or jury would think that an operation takes precautions for out-of-the-ordinary situations.

_____

_____

_____ 3. The Occupational Safety and Health Administration (OSHA) is the federal agency responsible for enforcing the Fair Labor Standards Act.

_____

_____

_____ 4. Chemicals can be considered physical hazards, health hazards, or both.

_____

_____

_____ 5. A Material Safety Data Sheet (MSDS) is required for all hazardous chemicals used in the workplace, and the sheets should be kept in a place where employees can access them.

_____

_____

_____ 6. A general safety audit is conducted to check proper fire drill procedures.

_____

_____

_____ 7. Personal protective equipment protects employees from potential hazards on the job.

_____

_____

_____ 8. An accident is a planned event that can cause property damage, injuries, time lost from work, or fatalities.

_____

_____

Part 2—Preventing Accidents and Injuries

_____ 1. One-half of all accidental fires in restaurants are due to faulty electrical wiring and equipment or improper equipment use.

_____

_____

_____ 2. To maintain safe conditions, it is important to keep all flammable items and materials away from heat sources such as ranges or hot water heaters.

_____

_____

_____ 3. There are three classes of fires: Class A, Class B, and Class C.

_____

_____

_____ 4. When using a fire extinguisher to put out a fire, use the PAST system.

_____

_____

_____ 5. The most important rule when deciding whether or not to fight a fire is to ask yourself, "Can I put it out without calling for help?"

_____

_____

_____ 6. The most serious type of burn is a first degree burn.

_____

_____

_____ 7. Grease and oil on floors are major causes of slips and falls and can occur anywhere.

_____

_____

_____ 8. When lifting a heavy item, it is important to always bend at the knees and not at the waist in order to prevent a back injury.

_____

_____

Part 3—First Aid and External Threats

_____ 1. Cardiopulmonary resuscitation (CPR) is used to restore breathing and heartbeat to an injured person who is not showing signs of breathing or a pulse.

_____

_____

_____ 2. The Heimlich maneuver is used when a person stops breathing due to an allergic reaction.

_____

_____

_____ 3. Someone who has been trained and has proper certification should only perform CPR and/or the Heimlich maneuver.

_____

_____

_____ 4. When providing first aid for a minor burn, the first thing that should be done is to place ice on the burned area.

_____

_____

_____ 5. After providing first aid for a cut, it is important to watch the cut for signs of infection.

_____

_____

_____ 6. Emergencies do not always mean an accident; another emergency might be a flood, fire, tornado, or other natural disaster.

_____

_____

_____ 7. An example of an external threat is arson.

_____

_____

_____ 8. Locking doors and windows when the facility is closed for business does not deter potential vandals or intruders.

_____

_____

Activity 3.2
Matching—Safety and the Law

Directions

Match the abbreviation or term to the correct description.

_____ OSHA	_____ MSDS	_____ Reasonable Care
_____ HCS	_____ Liability	_____ FLSA
_____ Safety Audit	_____ Emergency Plan	_____ PPE

A. The completed version of this is in the form of a checklist and is used to record the results of an inspection of the facilities, equipment, and employee and management practices

B. Are required for all hazardous chemicals used in the workplace

C. Ensures that young people do not risk their health or educational opportunities

D. A legal term that means an ordinary person would think the operation takes careful precautions

E. Personal protective equipment provided to employees to protect them from potential on-the-job hazards

F. Also known as "Right to Know" or HAZCOM

G. The federal agency responsible for creating and enforcing safety standards in the workplace

H. Created to protect workers, guests, and property in case of disaster or emergency

I. The legal responsibility that one person has to another

Activity 3.3
Report—School Fire Safety Plan

Directions

List the guidelines that you have learned to follow in the event of a fire at your school. Then further evaluate the fire safety of your school and classroom and prepare a short report of the information you collect.

Keep the following items in mind as you prepare your report:

- Identify the fire hazards in the classroom and at the school. How can these hazards be corrected?
- Locate extinguishers, identify their types, and check their expiration dates. Are they all in working order and located near potential trouble spots?
- Identify fire exits and fire alarm pulls.
- Identify procedures for communication and evacuation.

Take your notes in the space below. Attach additional pages as needed. Present your findings to the class.

_____

_____

_____

_____

_____

_____

_____

_____

_____

_____

_____

_____

_____

_____

_____

_____

_____

Activity 3.4
Write an Editorial—Preventing Accidental Fires Due to Electrical Equipment Failure

Directions

Write an editorial about the importance of checking electrical equipment and the causes of accidental fires in restaurants. Find statistics on the Internet that will support your case, for example, percent of fires caused by faulty electrical equipment, injuries, and steps that can be taken to prevent these types of accidents. Use the material in Section 3.2, "Preventing Accidents and Injuries," as a starting point for your search.

Take your notes in the space below. Present your findings to the class.

_____

_____

_____

_____

_____

_____

_____

_____

_____

_____

_____

_____

_____

_____

_____

_____

_____

_____

_____

_____

_____

Activity 3.5
Crossword Puzzle—Slips, Trips, and Falls

Directions

Complete the statements and answer the questions below. Use your answers to complete the crossword puzzle.

Across

1. A straight ladder should reach _____ _____ above the spot where it will rest.

3. _____ should be long enough so that you do not have to stand on the top step.

8. The number of people who are needed to safely hold a ladder is _____.

9. Proper floor cleaning procedures must be followed in order to prevent _____ _____.

11. _____ is something you should never do, even if you are in a hurry.

13. When there is a spill, have someone _____ the area.

15. _____ should be removed from the exterior of buildings after storms or high winds.

16. To help prevent slips and falls on ramps or stairs, _____ should be sturdy and secure.

19. Spills should be cleaned up _____.

21. _____ should be kept in good repair and cleaned regularly.

22. One of the three types of surfaces where slips, trips, and falls occur most often is _____.

Down

2. When using a ladder, work with someone who can _____ the bottom of it.

3. A common type of ladder is a _____ ladder.

4. Non-skid floor mats should be used in _____ _____ areas.

5. When a spill occurs, someone should _____ people around it.

6. _____ should fit smoothly and tightly to the floor.

7. When you are finished using a ladder, be sure to _____ it.

10. To prevent slips or falls near stairs or ramps, provide adequate _____.

12. Aisles in serving and dining areas should be _____ _____ wide.

14. When walking through a restaurant, be sure that chairs or tables do not block the _____.

17. Floors should be cleaned _____.

18. When using a ladder or stepstool, be sure to _____ the folding bar in place.

20. Ladders should be placed so that the person using it does not have to _____ to far to one side.

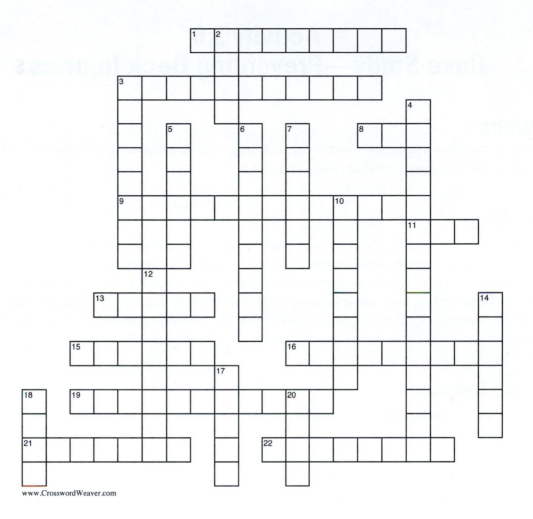

www.CrosswordWeaver.com

Activity 3.6
Case Study—Preventing Back Injuries

Directions

Read the case study below and think about the different things that Rob is doing in this situation. After reading the case study, answer the questions about Rob's behavior.

Case Study

Rob worked in at an ice cream shop after school and during the summer. Rob worked the front counter and was responsible for making ice cream cones and milk shakes. In addition to scooping ice cream, he also helped put stock away on delivery days. Many times, he would lift 5-gallon tubs of ice cream and put them in the freezer. About 6 months after starting work at the ice cream shop, Rob began to complain of back pain and went to see a doctor. The doctor explained that the pains could be related to Rob's lifting of the ice cream tubs. The doctor also warned Rob that this could become a chronic problem if something didn't change.

Case Study Questions

1. What are three things that could be causing back pain?

_____

_____

_____

_____

2. What can be done to correct this problem?

_____

_____

_____

_____

3. Why is it important to know about the causes of back problems?

_____

_____

_____

_____

_____

Activity 3.7
Poster/Presentation—Workplace Safety Guidelines

Directions

Brainstorm a list of workplace safety guidelines for your classroom kitchen with your classmates. Then, create a poster about a workplace-safety topic that has been assigned to you. When designing your poster, consider the following:

- Clarity of the message
- Persuasive effectiveness
- Use of emotion
- Use of graphic art and color
- Neatness
- Originality
- Technical accuracy

Take your notes in the space below. Use a separate sheet of paper, poster board, or computer to create your final poster.

_____

_____

_____

_____

_____

_____

_____

_____

_____

_____

_____

_____

_____

_____

_____

_____

_____

_____

Activity 3.8
Fill in the Blank—Knife Safety

Directions

Complete the statements below.

1. Keep knives _____.

2. Never touch _____ of knife blades.

3. When using a cutting board, place a damp cloth under it to prevent _____.

4. If interrupted when using a knife, be sure to put it down on a flat and _____ surface.

5. Never leave knives _____ under water.

6. If a knife _____, don't try to _____ it.

7. When carrying knives, always keep the _____ away from the body.

8. When passing a knife, place it on a sanitized surface and let the other person pick it up by the _____.

Activity 3.9
Matching—First Aid

Directions

Match the injury to the recommended first aid procedure.

_____ Minor burn   _____ Chemical burn

_____ Cuts and scrapes   _____ Choking

_____ Sprains and strains   _____ No pulse or breathing

_____ Muscle cramps   _____ Food allergy

A. If necessary, administer assistance with an EpiPen and notify health-care professionals immediately.

B. Cool the area and cover with a sterile gauze bandage.

C. Massage the affected area, then apply cold or heat and use an over-the-counter (OTC) pain reliever if needed.

D. Administer the Heimlich maneuver, if trained.

E. Stop the bleeding, clean the area, apply antibiotic, and cover the area.

F. Remove the cause, remove contaminated items, apply a cool damp cloth, and wrap the affected area loosely.

G. Rest, apply ice, apply compression, and keep the injured area elevated.

H. Administer CPR, if properly trained.

Activity 3.10
Mini Book—First Aid

Directions

Using the paper provided by your teacher or using a computer program, create a mini-book that can be used as a quick reference when working in the classroom, lab, or kitchen area. Your mini book should provide simple descriptions of common injuries (include a picture if available) on one page and the next page list the basic first aid steps and any first aid supplies that might be needed to treat the injury.

Use the chart on page 201 in *Chapter 3, Workplace Safety* as a guide.

Take your notes in the space below. Present your findings to the class.

_____

_____

_____

_____

_____

_____

_____

_____

_____

_____

_____

_____

_____

_____

_____

_____

_____

_____

_____

_____

_____

Chapter **4**

Activity 4.1
Test Your Professionalism and Understanding Standard Recipes IQ

Directions

Mark each of the following statements related to professionalism and understanding standard recipes as either true (T) or false (F). For each false statement, rewrite it to make it a true statement.

Part I—Professionalism

_____ 1. A culinarian is one who has studied and continues to study the art of cooking.

_____

_____

_____ 2. A professional is one who has a college degree, is unconcerned with their working environment, and is unable to maintain the standards of the workplace.

_____

_____

_____ 3. A culinary professional must create dishes that taste great; otherwise, customers will not return.

_____

_____

_____ 4. Sound judgment is a skill that can be learned in the classroom before beginning a professional career.

_____

_____

_____ 5. Personal responsibility means being accountable for the choices that you make.

_____

_____

_____ 6. The chef de cuisine is responsible for handling all the day-to-day operations in the kitchen.

_____

_____

_____ 7. The kitchen brigade system was created by Escoffier and has each kitchen employee performing a wide variety of tasks throughout the shift.

_____

_____

_____ 8. Scheduling employees is both an important and difficult part of a manager's job.

_____

_____

Part 2—Using Standardized Recipes

_____ 1. Math skills are not required in the professional kitchen.

_____

_____

_____ 2. The four basic math operations are addition, subtraction, multiplication, and division.

_____

_____

_____ 3. When working with fractions, the denominator is the upper part of the fraction and the numerator is the lower portion.

_____

_____

_____ 4. The commonly used system of measurement in the United States is metric units.

_____

_____

_____ 5. Metric units are based on multiples of 10.

_____

_____

_____ 6. To convert a temperature from Celsius (°C) to Fahrenheit (°F), subtract 32 from the Celsius number, multiply by 9, and then divide by 5.

_____

_____

_____ 7. The temperature at which water boils is 212°F (100°C).

_____

_____

_____ 8. The temperature at which water freezes is 23°F (-10°C).

Part 3—Standardized Recipes

_____ 1. A recipe works best when verbally shared from cook to cook.

_____

_____

_____ 2. A standard recipe follows a format that is clear for anyone to use.

_____

_____

_____ 3. Following a standard recipe allows the consistent production of good food.

_____

_____

_____ 4. After starting the recipe, complete all *mise en place*. *Mise en place* is a French term that means "clean as you go."

_____

_____

_____ 5. A recipe can be converted when the yield (amount provided by the recipe) is not the same as the amount needed.

_____

_____

_____ 6. The term volume, when used in a recipe, refers to the weight of an ingredient.

_____

_____

_____ 7. The edible portion (EP) refers to the amount of an item after it has been trimmed.

_____

_____

_____ 8. When costing a recipe, it is not always necessary to add the cost of common spices such as salt and pepper.

_____

_____

Activity 4.2
Professionalism Interview

Directions

Listen carefully to the presentation that will occur today regarding careers in the foodservice industry. Prior to the presentation, prepare several questions to ask that person about professionalism and the changing workforce. Be prepared to share what you learn with your classmates.

Sample Questions

1. What does it mean to be a culinary (foodservice) professional?

2. In your opinion, what are the five most important traits of a professional?

3. How do you stay knowledgeable in your field?

4. How do you train your staff to be professional?

5. Do you think customers notice if there is a lack of professionalism when they dine out?

6. How did you learn to discipline employees? How do you keep them motivated? Is it difficult to always use good judgment when making difficult decisions?

7. How do you demonstrate pride in your job?

8. How important is respect in the workplace?

Take your notes in the space below. Present your findings to the class.

_____

_____

_____

_____

_____

_____

_____

_____

_____

_____

_____

_____

_____

_____

Activity 4.3
Role-play—What Would You Do?

Directions

Read the scenario assigned to your group. Think about who the individuals are and how they might behave in the situation described. If you are not selected to role-play a scenario, think about how the classmates who are role-playing the scenario are portraying the characters and whether you would do things differently.

Scenario 1

Roles: Businessperson, Host/Hostess, Manager

A group of 10 business people have arrived for a 12:30 lunch reservation at Lucky's, a popular restaurant in the business community. They are celebrating three employee promotions and have made special arrangements prior to their arrival at the restaurant Their special arrangements included being seated in the "party room," pre-ordered appetizers so they could begin eating shortly after their arrival, and a special order for a double choco-late sheet cake layered with buttercream frosting that reads "Congratulations on Your Promotions" in blue icing, to be presented to the promoted employees after the meal. A hostess named Michelle (who is not working today) recorded the reservation and all the special arrangements a week earlier.

The businessperson who made all the arrangements approaches the host/hostess to let the restaurant know they have arrived and to confirm all the arrangements were made. Upon checking at the host/hostess stand, the businessperson finds that not only has the reservation been taken for the wrong time, but the cake says "Happy Birthday."

What happens next? Write your answer in the space below.

_____

_____

_____

_____

_____

_____

_____

_____

_____

_____

_____

_____

_____

Scenario 2

Roles: Host/Hostess, Manager, Customer 1, Customer 2, Customer 3

It is another busy Saturday night at Rupert's Diner. A group of three walks in and requests a table. They are told there is a 15-minute wait. The group is trying to make it to an 8:00 p.m. movie but decide to wait. After 15-minutes, the group still has not been seated and is becoming upset.

What happens next? Write your answer in the space below.

_____

_____

_____

_____

_____

_____

_____

_____

Scenario 3

Roles: Host/Hostess, Manager, Chef, and Family of Four

It is a busy Sunday brunch at the Café. A family of four arrives and requests a table and after a 20-minute wait they are seated. The family is greeted and the host/hostess explains the buffet to them. The family goes to the buffet line and returns to the table. As they begin to eat, one of the adults notices there is a hair in their eggs and the chicken is cold.

What happens next? Write your answer in the space below.

_____

_____

_____

_____

_____

_____

_____

Activity 4.4
Presentation—Kitchen Design

Directions

You have just been hired as the chef of a new family dining restaurant opening in town. This restaurant will seat 150 diners and will serve breakfast, lunch, and dinner. You have been asked to work with the general manager and architect to design the kitchen. Apply the concept of workstations to your kitchen design.

When designing the kitchen, be sure to include the following:

1. Emergency exit

2. Sink and dishwashing area

3. Hot food preparation area with at least three of the following stations:

 ■ Broiler

 ■ Fry

 ■ Grill

 ■ Sauté

 ■ Holding

4. Cold food preparation area

5. Dessert station

Use the area below to sketch your design. Use a separate sheet of paper, poster board, or your computer to create your final design.

Present your design to your classmates and explain your selection of equipment and placement of the stations.

Activity 4.5
Crossword Puzzle—Standardized Recipes

Directions

Complete the following statements and then use the answers to complete the crossword puzzle.

Across

2. To check the work on a _____ problem, simply add the number to the subtracted number.

6. The number placed outside the long division sign is called the _____.

7. The amount of product in its untrimmed form is referred to as the _____ _____ form.

9. The _____ is the upper portion of a fraction.

13. _____ is the metric measure of temperature.

15. _____ is a type of measure usually expressed in ounces and pounds.

16. _____ is a term that refers to how much of something is used in a recipe.

18. The _____ is an amount that is the same but expressed in different ways based on the unit of measure.

19. The number placed inside the long division sign is called the _____.

Down

1. To find the _____ _____ divide the desired yield by the original yield.

3. _____ __ _____, is a French term meaning "to put in place."

4. The amount of space an ingredient takes up is called the _____.

5. The _____ is the lower portion of a fraction.

8. A _____ is commonly expressed as parts per hundred.

10. The _____ _____ refers to product that has been cut and trimmed.

11. _____ is the customary measure of temperature.

12. A _____ is a written record of ingredients and the preparation steps needed to make a dish.

14. The total of several numbers added together is called the _____.

17. The _____ is the number of servings a recipe makes.

www.CrosswordWeaver.com

Activity 4.6
Mastering Measurement

Directions

Following is a list of measurement units. For each unit listed, complete Columns A, B, and C as described below:

1. In Column A, mark each measurement as either customary (C) or metric (M).

2. In Column B, write what is measured using that specific unit. The choices are volume (V), weight (W), temperature (T), or length (L).

3. In Column C, write the correct abbreviation for the measurement unit.

Measurement Unit	Column A (C or M)	Column B (V, W, T, or L)	Column C (Abbreviation)
1. Kilogram			
2. Cup			
3. Centimeter			
4. Quart			
5. Millimeter			
6. Ounce			
7. Tablespoon			
8. Meter			
9. Pint			
10. Milligram			
11. Fluid ounce			
12. Inches			
13. Degrees Fahrenheit			
14. Milliliter			
15. Teaspoon			
16. Gram			
17. Gallon			
18. Liter			
19. Pound			

Activity 4.7
Equivalent Measures

Directions

Following is a list of quantities. For each quantity listed, calculate it into its equivalent in the units listed.

1. 5½ cups = _____ ounces

2. 2½ pints = _____ ounces

3. 2 quarts, 6 ounces = _____ ounces

4. 2 quarts = _____ cups

5. 12 quarts = _____ gallons

6. 5 pounds = _____ ounces

7. 240 ounces = _____ pounds, _____ ounces

8. 3 quarts, 2 cups, 6 ounces = _____ ounces

9. 1 cup = _____ tablespoons

10. 9 teaspoons = _____ tablespoons

11. 16 cups = _____ quarts

12. 5¾ pounds = _____ ounces

13. 2 cups, 4 ounces = _____ ounces

14. 48 ounces = _____ cups

15. 144 ounces = _____ pounds

Activity 4.8
Recipe Conversion

Directions

Practice your recipe conversion skills by converting each recipe to reflect either an increased or decreased yield. Determine the conversion factor for each recipe and then complete the conversion.

Recipe 1: Poached Pears

Original Yield: 24 servings

New Yield: 12 servings

Serving Size: 1 each

Conversion Factor: _____

Original Ingredients	Converted Ingredients
24 Pears	___ Pears
2 qt Water	___ qt Water
3 lb Sugar	___ lb Sugar
4 tsp Vanilla	___ tsp Vanilla

Recipe 2: Beef Stroganoff

Original Yield: 6 portions

New Yield: 12 portions

Serving Size: 8 ounces

Conversion Factor: _____

Original Ingredients	Converted Ingredients
2 tbsp All-purpose flour	___ tbsp All-purpose flour
1 tsp Salt	___ tsp Salt
¼ tsp Pepper	___ tsp Pepper
3 lb Beef tenderloin, trimmed and cut into large dice	___ lb Beef tenderloin, trimmed and cut into large dice
4 tbsp Butter, oil, or other fat	___ tbsp Butter, oil, or other fat
3 cups Mushrooms, ¼ inch slices	___ cups Mushrooms, ¼-inch slices
1 cup Onions julienne	___ cups Onions, julienne
2 cloves Roasted garlic	___ cloves Roasted garlic
½ qt Brown stock	___ qt Brown stock
2 tbsp Tomato paste	___ tbsp Tomato paste
2 cups Sour cream	___ cups Sour cream

Recipe 3: Chicken Stir Fry

Original Yield: 4 Servings

New Yield: 12 servings

Serving size: 8 ounces

Conversion Factor: _____

Original Ingredients	Converted Ingredients
1 lb Boneless skinless chicken breasts	____ lb Boneless skinless chicken breasts
3 tbsp Cornstarch	____ tbsp Cornstarch
2 tbsp Reduced sodium soy sauce	____ tbsp Reduced sodium soy sauce
½ tsp Ginger, ground	____ tsp Ginger, ground
3 tbsp Vegetable oil	____ tbsp Vegetable oil
2 cups Broccoli florets	____ cups Broccoli florets
1 cup Celery, sliced	____ cups Celery, sliced
1 cup Carrots, thinly sliced	____ cups Carrots, thinly sliced
1 Onion, small and cut into wedges	____ Onions, small and cut into wedges
1 cup Reduced-sodium chicken stock or broth	____ cups Reduced-sodium chicken stock or broth

Recipe 4: Oatmeal Raisin Cookies

Original Yield: 12 dozen

New Yield: 36 dozen

Serving Size: 2 cookies

Conversion Factor: _____

Original Ingredients	Revised Ingredients
2¼ lb All-purpose flour	____ lb All-purpose flour
1 oz Baking soda	____ oz Baking soda
½ oz Cinnamon, ground	____ oz Cinnamon, ground
½ oz Salt	____ oz Salt
3 lb Butter, salted	____ lb Butter, salted
1 lb, 3 oz Sugar	____ lb, ____ oz Sugar
3½ lb Light brown sugar	____ lb Light brown sugar
10 Eggs	____ Eggs
1 fl oz Vanilla extract	____ oz Vanilla extract
3 lb, 3 oz Rolled oats	____ lb, ____ oz Rolled oats
1½ lb Raisins	____ lb Raisins

Activity 4.9
Determining Yields

Directions

It is important to order the correct amount of products when working in the kitchen. Many fruits and vegetables yield smaller amounts of useable product after they have been cleaned and trimmed. Complete the table below using the yield chart found on pp. 255-256 in *Chapter 4: Kitchen Essentials 1—Professionalism and Understanding Standard Recipes.*

Produce Item	Amount Needed for Recipe	Yield Percent	Actual Amount to Purchase
Cauliflower	3 lbs trimmed		
Zucchini	4 lbs trimmed		
Green beans	2 lbs trimmed		
Broccoli	5 lbs trimmed		
Okra	1½ lbs trimmed		
Black-eyed peas	2¾ lbs trimmed		
Eggplant (peeled)	3½ lbs		
Green pepper	1¾ lbs trimmed		
Corn on the cob	5 lbs		

Activity 4.10
Costing a Recipe—Gazpacho

Directions

Calculate the cost for each of the ingredients in the gazpacho recipe below. Use the table to record your calculations. Then, determine the cost per ounce and the cost per serving.

Gazpacho

Yield: 20 portions   Portion Size: 6 oz

Ingredient	Amount	Cost of Ingredient	Cost
Tomatoes	6¾ lbs	$2.45 per lb	
Cucumbers	64 oz	$9.50 per 15-lb box	
Onions	24 oz	$0.65 per lb	
Green bell peppers	1½ lbs	$ 3.18 per lb	
Crushed garlic	1 oz	$3.15 per lb	
Breadcrumbs	32 oz	$4.29 per 3 lb box	
Tomato juice	1¼ qt	$6.25 per ½ gal	
Red wine vinegar	8 oz	$2.75 per pt	
Olive oil	16 oz	$1.25 per cup	
Salt	To taste	$ 0.15 per recipe	
Pepper	To taste	$ 0.15 per recipe	
Lemon juice	5 tbsp	$ 0.25 per recipe	
		Total Cost	

1. Cost per ounce: _____

2. Cost per serving: _____

Chapter **5**

Activity 5.1
Test Your Foodservice Equipment and Techniques IQ

Directions

Mark each of the following statements related to equipment and techniques as either true (T) or false (F). For each false statement, rewrite it to make it a true statement.

Part 1—Foodservice Equipment

_____ 1. The receiving area is the last stop in the flow of food.

_____

_____

_____ 2. Dry goods such as flour, sugar, and grains should be stored at least 12 inches off the floor on wooden or plastic shelving.

_____

_____

_____ 3. A walk-in refrigerator or walk-in freezer is built directly into the foodservice facility itself.

_____

_____

_____ 4. A forged knife blade is made from a single piece of heated metal that is dropped into a mold and then hammered into the proper shape.

_____

_____

_____ 5. A chef's knife, also known as a French knife, is used to fabricate raw meat.

_____

_____

_____ 6. To keep knives in their best possible shape, they should be honed regularly.

_____

_____

_____ 7. Items such as a can opener, china cap, fish scaler, and a food mill are all considered cookware.

_____

_____

_____ 8. Holding and serving equipment can include bain-maries, steam tables, and espresso machines.

_____

_____

Part 2—Getting Ready to Cook

_____ 1. *Mise en place* refers to the preparation and assembly of ingredients, equipment, utensils, etc., that are needed for a particular dish or service.

_____

_____

_____ 2. When using most knives, you should place the food on the cutting board and then hold the handle of the knife with one hand and the blade of the knife with the other hand.

_____

_____

_____ 3. A seasoning is an ingredient used to change the primary flavor of a dish.

_____

_____

_____ 4. Flavor refers not only to the way a food tastes but also to its texture, appearance, doneness, and temperature.

_____

_____

_____ 5. Herbs and spices are used to enhance and add flavor to food.

_____

_____

_____ 6. When storing spices, it is important to store them near a heat source to slow down the loss of flavor and color.

_____

_____

_____ 7. Garlic belongs to the onion family.

_____

_____

_____ 8. Basic pre-preparation cooking techniques include searing steaks, creating gravies, and garnishing desserts.

_____

_____

Part 3—Cooking Methods

_____ 1. The three general types of heat cooking are dry-heat, moist-heat, and combination cooking.

_____

_____

_____ 2. Conduction does not require physical contact between the heat source and the food being cooked.

_____

_____

_____ 3. Roasting and baking are both examples of moist-heat cooking.

_____

_____

_____ 4. Sautéing is a method of cooking that uses a small amount of fat over a very high level of heat.

_____

_____

_____ 5. When frying foods, recovery time refers to the amount of time it takes for oil to reheat to the correct cooking temperature after food has been added.

_____

_____

_____ 6. Simmering, poaching, blanching, and steaming are all types of moist-heat cooking.

_____

_____

_____ 7. _Sous vide_ is a German term for underwater cooking.

_____

_____

_____ 8. To determine if food is done cooking, check the color and texture.

_____

_____

Activity 5.2
Know Your Knives

Directions

Identify each knife and explain its primary function in the kitchen.

	Knife Name	Function

Activity 5.3
Report/Presentation—Knife Care

Directions

Research the proper care and safety when using knives. Prepare a report that includes the following information:

- What are the tools needed to sharpen a knife?
- What are the different materials knives are made from?
- How does the care of a ceramic knife differ from that of a steel knife?
- What are the proper steps used in sharpening a knife?
- How should knives be stored?

Take your notes in the space below. Use a separate sheet of paper, poster board, or your computer to create your poster.

_____

_____

_____

_____

_____

_____

_____

_____

_____

_____

_____

_____

_____

_____

_____

_____

_____

_____

Activity 5.4
Crossword Puzzle—Foodservice Equipment

Directions
Complete the following statements and then use the answers to complete the crossword puzzle.

Across

1. A _____ is a medium to large pot made of heavy-weight material.

9. A _____ is a long-handled measuring utensil used to portion out liquids.

10. A _____ _____ is a shallow skillet with very short, slightly sloping sides.

11. A _____ is a manually operated slicer.

14. Steakhouses often use a _____ in place of a charcoal grill.

15. A _____ is a cooling unit that maintains temperatures between 32°F and 41°F.

16. A _____ _____ is used in the bake shop to cut and separate dough.

17. A _____ is made out of mesh-like material and comes in a variety of sizes.

Down

2. A _____ is used to shred the outer peel of citrus fruits.

3. A _____ is a special type of thermometer used to measure the temperature of many foods.

4. A _____ is used to drain liquids from cooked pasta and vegetables.

5. A small radiant oven used to brown foods is called a _____ and should not be confused with this lizard by the same name.

6. A _____ is often used for portioning out foods such as ice cream or butter.

7. A _____ _____ is also referred to as a melon baller and is used to scoop soft fruit and vegetables into balls.

8. A _____ _____ is used to beat and add air to light foods such as egg whites.

12. A _____ _____ is used for general cooking and has straight sides and a long handle.

13. A _____ is used to strain very fine items.

14. A _____ _____ gets its name from a foreign hat.

www.CrosswordWeaver.com

Activity 5.5
Basic Knife Cuts

Directions

Perform the *mise en place* for your station. Demonstrate the proper techniques for each of the following cuts. Be sure to check the size of each cut.

- Small dice   ¼ inch x ¼ inch x ¼ inch   Dice
- Medium dice   ½ inch x ½ inch x ½ inch   Dice
- Large dice   ¾ inch x ¾ inch x ¾ inch   Dice
- Julienne   ⅛ inch x ⅛ inch x 2½ inches   Stick cut
- Batonette   ¼ inch x ¼ inch x 2½–3 inches   Stick cut
- Brunoise   ⅛ inch x ⅛ inch x ⅛ inch   Dice

1. What was the most difficult part about this activity?

_____

_____

_____

2. Why is it important to have standard sizes for different cuts?

_____

_____

_____

3. Does it matter what type of knife is used for making these different cuts?

_____

_____

_____

4. Have you used any of these cuts before at home? On the job?

_____

_____

_____

Activity 5.6
Report/Presentation—Spotlight on Spices

Directions

Select an herb or spice from the following list. Prepare a short report, presentation, Web page, or display about the herb or spice you chose. Be sure to answer the questions listed below in your report and be prepared to share your findings with the class.

Herbs

Basil	Oregano
Bay leaves	Parsley
Chives	Peppermint
Cilantro	Rosemary
Dill	Sage
Lavender	Savory
Lemon grass	Spearmint
Marjoram	Tarragon
Mint leaves	Thyme

Spices

Allspice	Fennel
Anise	Ginger
Capers	Mace
Caraway	Mustard seeds
Cardamom	Nutmeg
Cayenne	Paprika
Chili pepper	Peppercorns
Cinnamon	Poppy seeds
Cloves	Saffron
Coriander	Sesame seeds
Cumin	Turmeric
Curry	Vanilla bean

Report/Presentation Questions

1. Where does the herb/spice come from?

2. What is the history of this herb/spice?

3. In what forms is this herb/spice most commonly used (whole, ground, dried, fresh, etc.)?

4. How is the flavor of this herb/spice described?

5. What does this herb/spice look like in its original form?

6. In what cultures, cuisines, or geographical areas is this herb/spice most commonly found?

7. What are the most common uses for this herb/spice?

8. What are some recipe examples that use this herb/spice?

9. How much does this herb/spice cost? Is it more or less expensive than other herbs/spices?

Take your notes in the space below. Use a separate sheet of paper, poster board, or your computer to create your poster.

_____

_____

_____

_____

_____

_____

_____

_____

_____

_____

_____

_____

_____

_____

_____

_____

_____

_____

_____

_____

_____

_____

_____

_____

_____

_____

_____

_____

_____

_____

Activity 5.7
Matching—Cooking Methods

Directions

The following is a list of cooking methods and their descriptions. For each method listed, complete Columns A and B as described below:

1. In Column A, mark each method as either a dry-heat cooking method (D), moist-heat cooking method (M), or combination cooking method (C).

2. In Column B, write the letter of the correct description of each cooking method on the right.

Cooking Method	Column A (D, M, or C)	Column B Description	Description
1. Bake			A. Cook food with waves of energy rather than with heat.
2. Shallow poach			B. Cook food in a closed oven without liquid.
3. Braise			C. Cook food using indirect heat in a closed environment (requires a longer cooking time than baking).
4. Broil			D. Cook food by placing it below a very hot heat source.
5. Stir fry			E. Cook food over, but not directly in, boiling liquid in a covered pot.
6. Deep fry			F. Cook food on a grill while basting with a marinade or sauce.
7. Poach			G. Sear food in hot oil, then cook tightly covered in a small amount of liquid, and finish in an oven or on the stovetop.
8. Grill			H. Cook food part-way in boiling water for a very short time.
9. Blanch			I. Cook food quickly in a small amount of fat or oil over high heat.
10. Sauté			J. Cook food on a rack above a heat source.
11. Pan fry			K. Cook food partially submerged in a liquid below the boiling point at temperatures of 180°F.
12. Steam			L. Cook breaded or batter-coated food by immersing it completely in hot fat or oil.
13. Microwave			M. Cook food in hot fat or oil over medium heat.
14. Roast			N. Cook food completely submerged in liquid below the boiling point at temperatures of 185°F to 205°F.
15. Boil			O. Cook food quickly in a small amount of fat or oil over high heat while stirring constantly.
16. Barbecue			P. Cook food submerged in a liquid that has reached the boiling point.
17. Simmer			Q. Sear bite-sized pieces of food, then cover them in liquid and simmer in a covered pot.
18. Stew			R. Cook food completely submerged in liquid below the boiling point at a temperature of 180°F.

1. With which cooking methods are you most familiar? Are there any methods that are new to you?

_____

_____

_____

_____

_____

_____

_____

2. Which cooking methods are used most often in your home?

_____

_____

_____

_____

_____

_____

_____

_____

_____

3. If you have a job, which cooking methods are used most often there?

_____

_____

_____

_____

_____

_____

_____

_____

_____

Activity 5.8
Presentation—Kitchen Equipment

Directions

Select four pieces of equipment from the following categories (only select one item from each category):

- Steamers
- Broilers
- Ranges, griddles, and fryers
- Ovens
- Holding and serving

Research the equipment that you have selected and include answers to the following questions in your presentation:

1. What is the primary function of this piece of equipment?
2. What are the main features of this piece of equipment?
3. What types of food items can be cooked, stored, or prepared using this piece of equipment?
4. What is the approximate cost of this piece of equipment?
5. What companies manufacture this equipment?
6. What does this piece of equipment look like?

Take your notes in the space below. Use a separate sheet of paper, poster board, or your computer to create your poster.

_____

_____

_____

_____

_____

_____

_____

_____

_____

_____

_____

Activity 5.9
Demonstration—Kitchen Essentials

Directions

You have been asked to present a lesson to a group of middle-school students about *mise en place*. You will have 3–5 minutes to explain the concept of *mise en place*, why it is important for a successful service, and then demonstrate one of the essential skills (this will be assigned to you by your instructor). During your demonstration, explain the steps as you are demonstrating them and include suggestions for making the process easier.

1. How important is it to practice the essential skills before demonstrating them to another student?

_____

_____

_____

_____

_____

_____

2. What was the most difficult part of this activity?

_____

_____

_____

_____

_____

_____

3. What would you have done differently?

_____

_____

_____

_____

_____

_____

Activity 5.10
Lab—Starting Out Simple

Directions

Getting comfortable in the kitchen starts with practicing the basics. In class, you have learned the importance of using standardized recipes, practicing effective *mise en place*, and learning safe and accurate knife skills. All of these contribute to the success of each recipe you make. Now it is time to see those skills in action.

Recipe Selection

- Baked Chicken
- Chicken Sauté with Onions, Garlic, and Basil
- Pepper Steak
- Poached Chicken Breast

Objectives

After completing this lab activity you should be able to:

- Identify the components and functions of a standard recipe
- Apply effective *mise en place* through practice
- Demonstrate basic preparation techniques
- Demonstrate proper use of liquid and dry measure tools
- Follow basic food safety and sanitation guidelines
- Follow basic safety guidelines to avoid causing injury to self or others

Directions

1. Review the recipe you have been assigned.
2. Perform *mise en place*. Plan for any substitutions or additional instructions you may have been given.
3. Prepare the recipe.
4. Clean up the area.

Baked Chicken

Yield: 6 servings

Measure	Ingredients
4 oz	Flour
2 tsp	Salt
½ tsp	White pepper
1 tsp	Hungarian paprika
½ tsp	Italian blend seasoning
18 pieces	Chicken (6 breasts, 6 legs, and 6 thighs)
1 lb	Melted butter, oil, or a mixture of butter and oil

Procedure

1. Combine flour with salt, white pepper, paprika, and Italian seasoning.

2. Pat chicken dry and dredge in flour mixture, shaking off excess.

3. Lightly coat in butter or oil and place on a sheet pan, skin-side up. Place dark meat on a separate pan.

4. Bake at 350°F for approximately 45 minutes or until an internal temperature of 165°F is reached.

Variations

Substitute a combination of Parmesan cheese, herbed breadcrumbs, and flour for original flour mixture.

Substitute various herbs for paprika and Italian blend seasoning.

© **Michael Zema, FMP/CCE. Used with permission.**

Chicken Sauté with Onions, Garlic, and Basil

Yield: 6 servings

Measure	Ingredients
6	Boneless, skinless chicken breasts
To taste	Salt
To taste	Pepper
As needed	Flour
6 oz	Clarified butter
2 oz	Onions, small dice
2 cloves	Fresh or roasted garlic, minced
3 oz	Tomato liquid or chicken stock
2 tsp	Lemon or other citrus juice
6 oz	Tomato *concassé*
12 oz	Chicken stock
5 leaves	Fresh basil, chiffonade

Procedure

1. Season chicken lightly with salt and pepper. Dredge in flour, shaking off excess.

2. Heat clarified butter in large sauté pan. Add chicken and brown on all sides. Do this in batches, making sure not to overcrowd pan. Remove from pan and reserve in warm place.

3. Add onions and garlic to pan and brown, adding additional clarified butter if necessary.

4. Deglaze the pan with tomato liquid or stock and lemon juice.

5. Add tomato *concassé* and chicken stock. Reduce to desired consistency.

6. Return chicken to pan and add basil. Simmer until chicken is cooked.

7. Adjust seasoning with salt and pepper.

© **Michael Zema, FMP/CCE. Used with permission.**

Pepper Steak

Yield: 6 servings

Measure	Ingredients
1 oz	Oil
2½ lb	Beef flank steak, trimmed and cut into strips
3 oz	Yellow onion, bâtonnet
1 clove	Roasted garlic, minced
1 lb	Tomatoes, medium dice
2 cups	Beef stock
2	Green bell peppers, bâtonnet
Slurry	
1 oz	Cornstarch
½ oz	Dark soy sauce
4 oz	Beef stock

Procedure

1. Heat oil in sauté pan. Add beef and brown on all sides.

2. Add onions and garlic; brown. Add tomatoes and continue sautéing until browned.

3. Deglaze the pan with a little bit of the stock. Add remaining stock and bring to a boil, skimming any impurities or excess fat off the top if necessary.

4. Reduce heat and simmer for 1 hour, or until meat is tender.

5. Add peppers and continue simmering until al dente.

6. Prepare slurry by dissolving cornstarch in soy sauce and beef stock. Slowly add mixture to sauté pan and allow to simmer for 5 minutes.

7. Adjust consistency if necessary by adding a little more stock if too thick, or by reducing if too thin.

8. Adjust seasoning with salt and pepper.

9. Serve with rice or pasta.

Variations

For different flavors, substitute regular tomatoes with fire-roasted or stewed varieties.

Shorten cooking time by marinating beef strips.

©Michael Zema, FMP/CCE. Used with permission.

Poached Chicken Breast

Yield: 6 servings

Measure	Ingredients
6	Boneless, skinless chicken breasts
As needed	Salt
As needed	Pepper
1 oz	Butter
1¼ qt	Chicken stock
1	Bay leaf
1 tsp	Italian blend seasoning
Roux	
1 oz	Butter
1 oz	Flour
4 oz	Heavy cream

Procedure

1. Lightly season chicken with salt and pepper.

2. Select a large sauté pan or two smaller pans that will accommodate all chicken breasts.

3. Rub the cold pan(s) with a light coating of butter. Place chicken in pan(s).

4. Add stock, bay leaf, and Italian seasoning to cover chicken.

5. Bring liquid to a boil and reduce to a simmer. Poach, turning once, until chicken is done, usually 8 to 10 minutes.

6. Remove from poaching liquid and reserve in warm place.

7. Create a roux by combining butter and flour (see procedure below).

8. Slowly add roux to the liquid until desired consistency is reached. Sauce will continue to thicken, so keep consistency on thin side.

9. Add cream until desired consistency is reached.

10. Strain sauce and return to pan(s).

11. Return chicken to pan, along with any liquid that has settled in holding pan. Correct temperature by lightly reheating.

Roux Procedure

1. Heat clarified butter or other fat in a heavy saucepan.

2. Add the flour and stir together with the fat to form a paste.

3. Cook the paste over medium heat until the desired color is reached.

4. Stir the roux continually to avoid burning.

© **Michael Zema, FMP/CCE. Used with permission.**

Chapter **6**

Activity 6.1
Test Your Knowledge of Stocks, Sauces, and Soups IQ

Directions

Mark each of the following statements related to stocks, sauces, and soups as either true (T) or false (F). For each false statement, rewrite it to make it a true statement.

Part 1—Stocks

_____ 1. Mirepoix is one of the four essential parts of stock and is made of coarsely chopped tomatoes, garlic, and basil to provide extra taste.

_____

_____

_____ 2. Bouquet garni is a French term meaning "bag of herbs" and is considered one of the aromatics used to flavor stock.

_____

_____

_____ 3. A stock is a flavorful liquid that is made by gently simmering bones and/or vegetables.

_____

_____

_____ 4. Court bouillon is an aromatic liquid made by simmering poultry, beef, or fish bones.

_____

_____

_____ 5. When preparing bones for use in stock, it is acceptable to "toss" them as is, into the stockpot.

_____

_____

_____ 6. When making stock, the ratio of liquid to flavoring ingredients is standard.

_____

_____

_____ 7. Degreasing is the process of removing fat that has cooled and hardened on the surface of the stock.

_____

_____

_____ 8. When cooling stock, it is important to follow good safety practices and limit the time the stock spends in the temperature danger zone.

_____

_____

Part 2—Sauces

_____ 1. A garde-manger chef is one who specializes in making sauces.

_____

_____

_____ 2. There are five classical grand sauces, which may also be called the "mother" sauces.

_____

_____

_____ 3. A roux is a thickener made of 3 parts cooked flour to 1 part fat.

_____

_____

_____ 4. A slurry can be used in place of roux and is made of cornstarch and cold liquid.

_____

_____

_____ 5. *Beurre manié* is a type of thickener used in hollandaise.

_____

_____

_____ 6. A liaison is a mixture of egg yolks and heavy cream used to finish sauces.

_____

_____

_____ 7. Sauces also can be made from the natural juices of meats.

_____

_____

_____ 8. You should never match the type of food you are serving to the sauce.

_____

_____

Part 3—Soups

_____ 1. The two basic kinds of soup are clear soups and thick soups.

_____

_____

_____ 2. *Oignon brûlé* is a raw onion that is added to stock to bring out the flavor.

_____

_____

_____ 3. The two types of thick soup are cream and purée.

_____

_____

_____ 4. Adding a slurry or roux to purée soups thickens them.

_____

_____

_____ 5. A bisque is a cream soup made from puréed shellfish shells.

_____

_____

_____ 6. It is important to boil cream soups to enhance the flavor.

_____

_____

_____ 7. Chowders are hearty, thick soups that are similar to cream soups.

_____

_____

_____ 8. Gazpacho and melon soups are best served hot.

_____

_____

Activity 6.2
Crossword Puzzle—Stocks

Directions

Complete the following statements and then use the answers to complete the crossword puzzle.

Across

3. This rich, lightly reduced stock is used as a glaze for roast meats and is called _____.

6. _____ is a glaze made from reduced stock and has a jelly-like consistency.

9. _____ _____ is similar to a bouquet garni but actually used in a bag.

10. _____ comes from a French word that refers to a mixture of coarsely chopped onions, carrots, and celery.

12. _____ is considered one of the chef's building blocks.

13. An aromatic vegetable broth is known as _____ _____.

14. _____ is a method used for preparing bones to be used in stock.

Down

1. _____ is similar to fish stock, is very flavorful, and made from fish bones.

2. _____ is the process used to remove fat from cooled stock.

4. A weak stock made from reused bones is called _____.

5. A French term for a "bag of herbs" that includes thyme, parsley stems, and bay leaf tied together is called a _____ _____.

7. _____ is a process used to quickly cook bones for stock.

8. Herbs, spices, and flavorings used to create a savory smell in stocks are known as _____.

11. _____ is another name for broth.

www.CrosswordWeaver.com

Activity 6.3
Lab—Making a Basic Stock

Directions

Preparing stocks is a cost-effective way to use valuable trimmings from vegetables, meat, or fish. Stocks also form the base for many delicious and popular soups. Put your skills to the test by preparing these classic recipes.

Recipe Selection

- Basic Brown Stock
- Basic White Stock
- Fish Stock

Objectives

After completing this lab activity you should be able to:

- Apply effective *mise en place* through practice
- Demonstrate proper use of equipment and tools
- Follow basic food safety and sanitation guidelines
- Follow basic safety guidelines to avoid causing injury to self or others
- Prepare ingredients for and cook different types of stocks

Directions

1. Review the recipe you have been assigned.
2. Perform *mise en place*. Plan for any substitutions or additional instructions you may have been given.
3. Prepare the recipe.
4. Clean up the area.

Basic Brown Stock

Yield: 1 gallon

Measure	Ingredients
10 lb	Beef or veal bones
6 qt	Cold water
8 oz	Onions, large dice
4 oz	Carrots, large dice
4 oz	Celery, large dice
2 cloves	Garlic, minced
3 oz	Tomato paste
3 oz	Tomato purée
Sachet	
1	Bay leaf
¼ tsp	Fresh thyme
5	Black peppercorns
3	Parsley stems
2	Whole cloves

Procedure

1. Brown bones thoroughly in a roasting pan at 375°F for 30 to 45 minutes.

2. Remove bones from pan; reserve pan. Place bones in a large stockpot and cover with water. Allow liquid to come to a boil, quickly reduce to a simmer. Skim the surface to remove any impurities as necessary and continue to simmer for 2 to 3 hours.

3. Add onions, carrots, celery, and garlic (mirepoix) to roasting pan, making sure there is a sufficient amount of fat to coat. Return to oven and brown thoroughly.

4. Add tomato paste and purée and brown for 5 to 7 minutes.

5. Deglaze roasting pan with some of the simmering liquid from the stockpot.

6. After bones have simmered for 2 to 3 hours, add browned mirepoix and sachet. Simmer an additional 2 to 3 hours.

7. Continue to occasionally skim surface of stock with a disposable paper towel.

8. When done, strain through a china cap and again through another china cap lined with a damp cheesecloth. This double process is actually quicker than straining through a cheesecloth-lined china cap first.

9. Refrigerate and cool stock quickly.

Notes

There are differing opinions regarding the length of time to simmer a stock. As a rule of thumb, smaller bones require a shorter simmering time.

If stock will not be used within 2 to 3 days, freeze it. Bring stock up to a quick boil and simmer 10 minutes every 3 days if kept in the cooler. This method helps minimize bacteria growth and improves flavor.

© **Michael Zema, FMP/CCE. Used with permission.**

Basic White Stock

Yield: 1 gallon

Measure	Ingredients
10 lb	Chicken, veal, or beef bones
6 qt	Cold water
8 oz	Onions, large dice
4 oz	Carrots, large dice
4 oz	Celery, large dice
2 cloves	Garlic, chopped
Sachet	
1	Bay leaf
¼ tsp	Fresh thyme
5	Black peppercorns
5	Fresh parsley stems
2	Whole cloves

Procedure

1. Rinse bones and place in a large stockpot with water. Bring to a boil and quickly reduce to a simmer. Skim the surface to remove any impurities as necessary and continue to simmer for 2 to 3 hours.

2. Add onions, carrots, celery, garlic (mirepoix), and sachet and continue to simmer an additional 2 hours.

3. Occasionally continue to skim the surface with a disposable paper towel.

4. When done, strain through a china cap and again through another china cap lined with a damp cheese-cloth. This double process is actually quicker than straining through a cheesecloth-lined china cap first.

5. Refrigerate and cool stock quickly.

Notes

There are differing opinions regarding the length of time to simmer a stock. As a rule of thumb, smaller bones require a shorter simmering time.

If stock will not be used within 2 to 3 days, freeze it. Bring stock up to a quick boil and simmer 10 minutes every 3 days if kept in the cooler. This method helps minimize bacteria growth and improves flavor.

© Michael Zema, FMP/CCE. Used with permission.

Fish Stock

Yield: 1 gallon

Measure	Ingredients
10 lb	Fish bones, coarse cut
8 oz	Onions, medium dice
4 oz	Celery, medium dice
2 oz	Leeks, medium dice
2 oz	Carrots, medium dice
2 cloves	Garlic, minced
1	Bay leaf
¼ tsp	Thyme
4	Black peppercorns
4	Parsley stems
2	Whole cloves
2 oz	Lemon juice
6 qt	Cold water

Procedure

1. Sweat all ingredients in a stockpot except water and lemon juice.

2. Deglaze pot with lemon juice. Add the water, bring to a boil, and reduce to a simmer.

3. Skim stock with a clean paper towel to remove excess impurities and fat, without removing the herbs and spices.

4. Simmer for 45 minutes. Taste and continue to simmer if necessary to reach desired flavor.

5. Strain through a china cap and again through a china cap lined with a damp cheesecloth. This double process is quicker than straining once through a cheesecloth-lined china cap.

6. Cool stock quickly and refrigerate. If stock will not be used within 1 to 2 days, then freeze.

Notes

As a rule of thumb, bring stock up to a quick boil and simmer 10 minutes every 3 days if kept in the cooler. This method helps to minimize bacteria growth and improves flavor.

© Michael Zema, FMP/CCE. Used with permission.

Activity 6.4
Poster/Presentation—The Mother Sauces

Directions

You work for a local restaurant and have been asked to present a series of seminars on the mother sauces. Your team has been chosen to create an informational poster describing the history of the sauce, recipes using the sauce, and sauces that are derived from the mother sauce. Each poster should include images showing how to make the sauce and how home cooks can make the sauce on their own.

You may choose from one of the following sauces:

- Béchamel
- Velouté
- Brown or *Espagnole*
- Tomato
- Hollandaise

Part 1—Design a Poster

Working with your team, research your sauce and find recipes that you can share that are made from your sauce.

Refer to *Chapter 6: Stocks, Sauces, and Soups* in your textbook for information and also refer to cookbooks and the Internet for information.

You may use the space provided below to draw a draft of your poster. Create your final poster using another medium (poster board, computer, etc.).

Part 2—Develop and Deliver a Presentation

Design your presentation to answer the following questions:

1. What is the history of your sauce?

_____

_____

_____

_____

2. What are some famous recipes that this sauce is used in?

_____

_____

_____

_____

3. What are some hints for making this sauce?

_____

_____

_____

_____

4. What are some derivatives of this sauce?

_____

_____

_____

_____

5. Why did you choose this sauce?

_____

_____

_____

_____

Activity 6.5
Internet Activity—Cooking with Roux

Directions

Research roux on the Internet. In your research, answer the following questions:

1. How is roux traditionally made?

2. What are alternatives to a traditional roux?

3. How many different types of roux are there?

4. Find at least two recipes that use roux. Each recipe should use a different type of roux or roux alternative.

5. Which types of cuisine most often use roux? Include a recipe from one of these cuisines.

Use the space below to take your notes. Attach additional pages as necessary.

_____

_____

_____

_____

_____

_____

_____

_____

_____

_____

_____

_____

_____

_____

_____

_____

_____

_____

Activity 6.6
Mini Book—Sauces Around the World

Directions

Research various sauces from around the world and then select five sauces from five different cultures. Then, create a mini book that includes the following components:

- Name of the country/culture
- Sauce selected
- Recipe using that sauce
- Picture of the dish made with that sauce
- Two to three interesting facts about the sauce

Using the paper provided or using a computer program, create a mini book that can be used as a reference when working in the kitchen or that can be shared with another student.

1. What was the most surprising thing you learned about your sauces?

_____

_____

_____

2. Why did you select the culture/countries that you did?

_____

_____

_____

3. Did you select from traditions that you knew about or did you choose to learn about different cultures?

_____

_____

_____

4. Why is it important to know about culinary traditions from around the world?

_____

_____

_____

Activity 6.7
Create a Soup Recipe

Directions

Today you are in charge of creating the Soup of the Day. Using what you have learned about creating soups and stocks from this unit, your job is to create a new soup recipe—either a twist on a classic soup or something of your own creation. To successfully complete this task you will need to:

- Determine if this is a hot or cold soup
- How many servings
- List of ingredients
- Steps of preparation
- Final presentation
- Complete a written version of the recipe

Part 1

Decide the type of soup and the name of the soup. Determine the list of ingredients along with the amounts needed.

Part 2

Test the recipe, either in the lab or at home. Make adjustments to the recipe as needed until the desired flavor is achieved.

Part 3

Write down the ingredients and the steps used to create the soup.

Part 4 (Optional)

Prepare and serve to the class.

Use the space below to take your notes. Attach additional pages as necessary.

_____

_____

_____

_____

_____

_____

Activity 6.8
Lab—Hot Soups

Directions

Preparing soups is a cost-effective way to use valuable trimmings from vegetables, meat, or fish. Many delicious and popular soups are made from stocks. Put your skills to the test by preparing these classic recipes.

Recipe Selection

- New England Clam Chowder
- Onion Soup
- Roasted Winter Squash Soup
- Shrimp Bisque

Objectives

After completing this lab activity you should be able to:

- Apply effective *mise en place* through practice
- Demonstrate proper use of equipment and tools
- Follow basic food safety and sanitation guidelines
- Follow basic safety guidelines to avoid causing injury to self or others
- Prepare ingredients for and cook different types of soups

Directions

1. Review the recipe you have been assigned.
2. Perform *mise en place*. Plan for any substitutions or additional instructions you may have been given.
3. Prepare the recipe.
4. Clean up the area.

Onion Soup

Yield: 32 ounces

Measure	Ingredients
2 oz	Butter
2 oz	Olive oil
8 oz	Onions, julienned
1 tsp	Italian-blend seasoning
20 oz	Chicken stock
20 oz	Beef stock
To taste	Salt
To taste	Pepper

Procedure

1. Heat butter and olive oil. Add onions and sauté until caramelized (golden-brown onions add extra flavor and sweetness). Add Italian seasoning and sweat for 2 minutes.

2. Add a little stock to deglaze pan. Add remaining stock and simmer for 20 minutes.

3. Adjust flavor with salt and pepper.

Variation

French Onion Soup

Top bowl of soup with a seasoned crouton topped with gruyere, Parmesan, or asiago cheese (a combination can be used). Place under broiler to melt the cheese. Garnish with parsley and/or paprika.

© **Michael Zema, FMP/CCE. Used with permission.**

New England Clam Chowder

Yield: 32 ounces

Measure	Ingredients
2 oz	Unsalted butter
2 oz	Bacon, minced
4 oz	Onions, small dice
2 oz	Celery, small dice
4 oz	Potatoes, small dice
3 oz	Flour
12 oz	Canned clams
8 oz	Clam juice
12 oz	Low-fat milk
To taste	Clam base
As needed	Fresh chives, snipped

Procedure

1. Melt butter; add bacon, and sauté, making sure the bacon is not too crisp.

2. Add onions, celery, and potatoes, sautéing until al dente.

3. Add flour to make a roux, using only enough flour to absorb excess fat in pan. Cook for 10 minutes.

4. Temper milk. Add clams, clam juice, and tempered milk. Continue to simmer until potatoes are cooked.

5. Adjust flavor with clam base.

6. Serve in warm bowl or cup and garnish with chives.

© **Michael Zema, FMP/CCE. Used with permission.**

Roasted Winter Squash Soup

Yield: 8 servings

Measure	Ingredients
3 lb	Winter squash (a mixture of pumpkin, acorn, or butternut squash can be used)
As needed	Olive or pumpkin seed oil
2 oz	Butter or oil
1 large	Onion, small dice
6 oz	Carrots, small dice
1	Leek, white part only, cleaned, small dice
4 oz	Celery, small dice
1 clove	Garlic, minced
48 oz	Chicken or vegetable stock
4 oz	Heavy cream
To taste	Salt
To taste	Pepper
As needed	Sour cream

Procedure

1. Cut squash in half and scoop out seeds, reserving for garnish if desired. Brush with mixture of olive oil and/or pumpkin seed oil. Place upside down on sheet pan.

2. Slow roast squash in a 275°F oven for 2 hours or until pulp is tender. Scoop out pulp and reserve, discarding skin.

3. Sauté onions, carrots, leeks, celery, and garlic in a heavy saucepan until tender.

4. Add roasted squash pulp and a little stock to deglaze the pan. Add remaining stock and simmer for 7 to 10 minutes.

5. Using a hand blender/processor, process soup until a smooth texture is reached.

6. Add cream to adjust consistency. Stock can also be used to adjust consistency.

7. Adjust seasoning with salt and pepper.

8. At service, garnish with roasted, chopped pumpkin seeds, if desired. Drizzle a little sour cream on top for flavor and color, if desired.

© **Michael Zema, FMP/CCE. Used with permission.**

Shrimp Bisque

Yield: 8 servings

Measure	Ingredients
3 oz	Butter, oil, or other fat
3 oz	Shallots, minced
1 tbsp	Garlic, minced
3 oz	Flour
3 oz	Fish stock
2 qt	1% low-fat milk
6 oz	Shrimp
As needed	Shrimp paste
To taste	Pepper
As needed	Deep fried shallots

Procedure

1. Heat butter or oil. Add shallots and garlic, and sauté until translucent.

2. Whisk in enough flour to make a blonde roux. Cook for 8 to 10 minutes.

3. Add stock to deglaze pan and reduce by ¾.

4. Temper milk. Add tempered milk and shrimp and simmer for 15 minutes.

5. Adjust flavor with shrimp paste and pepper if needed.

6. Garnish with deep fried shallots.

© **Michael Zema, FMP/CCE. Used with permission.**

Activity 6.9
Lab—Cold Soups

Directions

Cold soups are often served as appetizers or served on a hot day. Fruit soups are made using fresh seasonal fruits, while other soups, such as gazpacho, use vegetables.

Recipe Selection

- Peach and Yogurt Soup
- Gazpacho
- Strawberry Soup

Objectives

After completing this lab activity you should be able to:

- Apply effective *mise en place* through practice
- Demonstrate proper use of equipment and tools
- Follow basic food safety and sanitation guidelines
- Follow basic safety guidelines to avoid causing injury to self or others
- Prepare ingredients for and cook different types of soups

Directions

1. Review the recipe you have been assigned.
2. Perform *mise en place*. Plan for any substitutions or additional instructions you may have been given.
3. Prepare the recipe.
4. Clean up the area.

Peach and Yogurt Soup

Yield: 4 servings

Measure	Ingredients
16 oz	Fresh or canned peaches (follow appropriate method)
12 oz	Fruit acidity (citrus, orange, or other juice)
4 oz	Chicken stock
2 oz	Honey or pancake syrup
¼ tsp	Ground cinnamon
4 oz	Plain yogurt
As needed	Heavy cream

Procedure

Fresh Peaches

1. Pit and coarsely chop peaches (do not peel).

2. Bring fruit acidity and honey to simmer. Add peaches and simmer until tender.

3. Remove from heat, allow to cool, and process. Add yogurt and cinnamon, and process for another minute.

4. Adjust consistency to desired thickness with heavy cream.

Canned Peaches

1. Omit 12 ounces fruit acidity. Process canned peaches, honey, 1 ounce of the fruit acidity, cinnamon, and yogurt until a smooth texture is reached. Add some of the can liquid for flavor and consistency.

2. Add heavy cream if needed to adjust texture and consistency.

Suggestion

Serve in cold bowls/cups and garnish with mint and/or pistachios.

© Michael Zema, FMP/CCE. Used with permission.

Gazpacho

Yield: 4 servings

Measure	Ingredients
1 cup	Italian dressing
48 oz	V8-Vegetable juice
1	Green pepper, medium dice
½	Cucumber, small dice
To taste	Cilantro
1	Large tomato, medium dice
To taste	Cracked pepper
As needed	Shrimp

Procedure

1. Pour all of the vegetable juice into a large pan.

2. Dice the green pepper and toss out the seeds.

3. Dice the cucumber.

4. Dice the tomato.

5. Dice the cilantro.

6. Place all the vegetables into the pan.

7. Add the Italian dressing.

8. Add pepper to taste

9. Chill for 24 hours. Garnish with shrimp and/or cucumber slices.

This recipe is licensed under a Creative Commons Attribution Share Alike 3.0 License.

http://www.opensourcefood.com/people/Seba/recipes/gazpacho

Strawberry Soup

Yield: 4 servings

Measure	Ingredients
1½ cups	Cold water
¾ cup	Citrus juice (orange, lemon, or similar)
½ cup	Sugar
2 tbsp	Fresh lemon juice
1	Stick cinnamon
2 qt.	Strawberries, hulled and puréed
1 cup	Heavy cream
¼ cup	Sour cream

Procedure

1. Combine water, fruit juice, sugar, lemon juice, and cinnamon stick in a large saucepan.

2. Boil, uncovered, about 17 minutes stirring constantly.

3. Add strawberry purée and continue boiling, stirring frequently.

4. Discard cinnamon stick and cool cooked mixture.

5. Whip cream and stir in sour cream.

6. Fold into strawberry mixture.

7. Refrigerate for 6 to 8 hours.

8. When ready to serve, garnish with whole strawberries.

Activity 6.10
Lab—Classic Sauces

Directions

A well-made sauce is the mark of a good chef. Sauces often provide the finishing touch to a dish and provide extra flavor. Try some of these classic sauces, which form the base for almost every other sauce used in the kitchen.

Recipe Selection

- Béchamel Sauce
- Brown Sauce
- Hollandaise Sauce
- Tomato Sauce
- Velouté Sauce

Objectives

After completing this lab activity you should be able to:

- Apply effective *mise en place* through practice
- Demonstrate proper use of equipment and tools
- Follow basic food safety and sanitation guidelines
- Follow basic safety guidelines to avoid causing injury to self or others
- Prepare ingredients for and cook different types of sauces

Directions

1. Review the recipe you have been assigned.
2. Perform *mise en place*. Plan for any substitutions or additional instructions you may have been given.
3. Prepare the recipe.
4. Clean up the area.

Béchamel Sauce

Yield: 1 quart

Measure	Ingredients
2 oz	Oil, butter, or other fat
½ oz	Onions, medium dice
½	Bay leaf
1	Whole clove
1	Sprig fresh thyme
2 oz	Flour
1 qt	Milk, heated
To taste	Salt
To taste	Pepper
To taste	Nutmeg

Procedure

1. Heat oil or butter. Add onions, bay leaf, clove, and thyme. Sweat until onions are translucent.

2. Add flour to make a roux.

3. Slowly whisk milk into the roux, beating constantly, and simmer for 20 to 30 minutes, periodically skimming surface.

4. Season lightly with salt, pepper, and nutmeg.

5. Strain through a china cap, straining a second time through a china cap (*chinois*) if necessary. Cool.

6. Sauce should be the consistency of heavy cream.

© **Michael Zema, FMP/CCE. Used with permission.**

Brown Sauce

Yield: 2 quarts

Measure	Ingredients
8 oz	Mirepoix
3 oz	Oil, butter, or other fat
3 oz	Flour
2 oz	Tomato paste
5 pts	Basic brown stock
½	Sachet

Procedure

1. Brown mirepoix in oil or butter.

2. Slowly add flour, making sure to absorb all fat and coat mirepoix thoroughly. Cook for 8 to 10 minutes.

3. Add tomato paste and continue to caramelize.

4. Add a small amount of stock to deglaze pan.

5. Add remaining stock and sachet. Simmer for 1 hour, skimming surface of any impurities as necessary.

6. Strain through a china cap (*chinois*). Serve or refrigerate.

© **Michael Zema, FMP/CCE. Used with permission.**

Hollandaise Sauce

Yield: 16 ounces

Measure	Ingredients
⅛ tsp	Black peppercorns, crushed
1½ oz	White wine vinegar
To taste	Salt
2 tbsp	Lemon juice, divided
1 oz	Cold water
5	Egg yolks
12 oz	Clarified butter
To taste	Lemon juice
To taste	Cayenne pepper

Procedure:

1. Combine peppercorns, vinegar, salt, 1 tablespoon lemon juice, and reduce *au sec* (until dry).

2. Remove from heat and add water to cool reduction.

3. Transfer reduction to stainless steel bowls.

4. Whisk in egg yolks.

5. Return to heat and continue to whisk in yolks until thick.

6. Begin to add a little bit of clarified butter at a time. Continue to add butter until desired consistency is reached.

7. Adjust seasoning with lemon juice, salt, and cayenne pepper.

8. If sauce is too thick, add a little warm water.

9. If desired, strain through cheesecloth.

10. Serve warm or hold for a maximum of 1½ hours.

© Michael Zema, FMP/CCE. Used with permission.

Tomato Sauce

Yield: 2 quarts

Measure	Ingredients
2 oz	Olive oil
4 oz	Onions, small dice
2 tbsp	Italian-blend seasoning
2 cloves	Garlic, minced
3½ lb	Tomatoes
1 cup	Tomato purée
½ cup	Fresh basil, chopped
To taste	Salt
To taste	Pepper

Procedure

1. Heat olive oil. Sweat onions, garlic, and Italian seasoning.

2. Add tomatoes and tomato purée and allow to caramelize. Then, simmer for 30 minutes.

3. Add basil and simmer for another 10 minutes.

4. Adjust flavor with salt and pepper.

© Michael Zema, FMP/CCE. Used with permission.

Velouté Sauce

Yield: 1 quart

Measure	Ingredients
2 oz	Butter, oil, or other fat
2 oz	Flour
40 oz	White stock
To taste	Salt
To taste	Pepper

Procedure:

1. Heat butter or oil in saucepan and slowly add flour to make a roux.

2. Slowly add stock and simmer for 15 minutes, reducing sauce by 6 to 8 ounces.

3. Skim surface as necessary to remove any impurities.

4. Strain through a china cap (*chinois*).

5. Adjust seasoning with salt and pepper.

6. Sauce should be consistency of heavy cream.

© Michael Zema, FMP/CCE. Used with permission.

Chapter **7**

Activity 7.1
Test Your Communication IQ

Directions

Mark each of the following statements related to communication as either true (T) or false (F). For each answer that is false, rewrite it to make it true.

Part 1—The Communication Process

_____ 1. Communication is the process of sending and receiving information electronically by cell phone, text message, or social networking sites.

_____

_____

_____ 2. A communication has five parts: sender, receiver, message content, message channel, and context.

_____

_____

_____ 3. The sender begins the communication process and must determine the best way to send the message.

_____

_____

_____ 4. Barriers to communication are rarely present in the communication process.

_____

_____

_____ 5. Using jargon is one method used to ensure effective communication.

_____

_____

_____ 6. When communicating, it is important to understand the nonverbal message in addition to the words that are spoken.

_____

_____

_____ 7. Nonverbal communication includes touch, eye contact, gestures, posture, and facial expressions.

_____

_____

_____ 8. Nonverbal gestures mean the same thing in every culture.

_____

_____

Part 2—Communication Skills

_____ 1. Messages may be subject to interpretation based on the receiver's experience, background, and other factors.

_____

_____

_____ 2. In the restaurant and foodservice industry, it is important for guests to find the employees credible.

_____

_____

_____ 3. When listening to speakers, it is a good idea to finish their sentences for them.

_____

_____

_____ 4. A good speaker rarely interacts with the audience, uses buzzwords, and speaks in a monotone.

_____

_____

_____ 5. When speaking on the phone, it is a good idea to take notes if the caller has a large amount of information to share with you.

_____

_____

_____ 6. Written messages are often more formal than speaking.

_____

_____

_____ 7. When writing in the workplace, it is acceptable to use abbreviations commonly used in text messages.

_____

_____

_____ 8. To make professional written communication easier to understand, use proper grammar, spelling, and punctuation.

_____

_____

Part 3—Types of Communication

_____ 1. A mission statement describes the company's purpose and key objectives to the team and its owners.

_____

_____

_____ 2. A vision statement defines the company's financial goals.

_____

_____

_____ 3. Interpersonal communication is any two-way communication that has delayed feedback and only occurs between friends and family.

_____

_____

_____ 4. Actions are as important in building trust as the conversation can be.

_____

_____

_____ 5. Empathy is the act of identifying with the feelings, thoughts, or attitudes of another person.

_____

_____

_____ 6. Successful managers will use a variety of communication methods to communicate with their staff and coworkers.

_____

_____

_____ 7. Coaching is a technique that should only be used when an employee is in danger of being fired.

_____

_____

_____ 8. When correcting employee behavior it's best to wait for several days after the incident happened.

_____

_____

Activity 7.2
The Communication Process—Do You Understand Me?

Directions

Part 1

During this exercise you will be creating a paper model. You are not allowed to ask questions or look at what any of your classmates are doing. Follow your teacher's directions exactly as he or she says them. You should each have a piece of plain white paper; place it on the desk/table in front of you before the teacher begins.

Close your eyes. No talking or peeking. Listen to and follow the directions that your teacher gives you.

When your teacher is done giving the directions, open your eyes and unfold your paper. Compare your results to the person next to you. Do they look the same or different? What happened?

Write your responses in the space below. Present your findings to the class.

_____

_____

_____

_____

_____

_____

_____

_____

_____

_____

_____

_____

_____

_____

_____

_____

_____

Part 2

This time you are going to repeat the activity, but you can ask your teacher questions if you need to.

Compare your results to the person next to you. Do they look similar or different? How was this time different from the first? What changed? Which set of instructions provided the better result?

Write your responses in the space below. Present your findings to the class.

_____

_____

_____

_____

_____

_____

_____

_____

_____

_____

_____

_____

_____

_____

_____

_____

_____

_____

_____

_____

_____

_____

_____

Activity 7.3
Role-play—Communication Breakdown in the Kitchen

Directions

Read the scenario assigned to your group. Think about who the individuals are and how they might behave in the situation described. If you are not selected to role-play this scenario, think about how the classmates who are role-playing the scenario are portraying the characters and whether you would do things differently.

Scenario 1

Roles: Cook, Server

It's a busy Saturday evening at the local café and the hostess has put the dining room on a 30-minute wait until more tables open up. Mary, the server, has rung in an order for a party of six and there are several special requests. She notes those on the check but also goes into the kitchen to talk to the cook. When she enters the kitchen, Joe, the cook, is working hard on the grill line. The kitchen is noisy with several servers, cooks, and dishwashers all going about their business.

Mary approaches the hot line and begins listing all of the special changes that need to be made to her order. Joe nods his head but continues working on the plates that he is getting ready to put up. When Joe does get to Mary's order, he can't remember what she said.

What happens next? Write your answer in the space below.

Scenario 2

Roles: Dishwasher, Cook

It's another busy Sunday brunch at the Wildflower Café. Two dishwashers have called in sick and the lone dishwasher who came in is trying hard to keep clean pots and pans for the cook while also running the dish machine.

Working at the dish machine is very noisy and it's difficult to hear when someone is speaking. In addition, there is a loud radio playing in the background to help motivate the dishwashers. The cook approaches the dishwasher and asks for more plates. The dishwasher nods his or her head and keeps working.

What happens next? Write your answer in the space below.

_____

_____

_____

_____

_____

_____

_____

Scenario 3

Roles: Server, Manager, Family of Three

It's mid-afternoon on a Friday and the lunch crowd has left. The day shift is working on side work and getting ready for the end of the shift. The manager seats the family of three in a section that is about to be closed for the end of the shift. The manager then goes to his or her office to work on paperwork. Several minutes pass before the server notices the table.

The server approaches the table and asks the family, "What do you want?" The server does not write down the order. The order is placed, and about 10 minutes later the food is ready to be served. When the order is brought to the table, there are several problems with the order.

What happens next? Write your answer in the space below.

_____

_____

_____

_____

_____

_____

_____

Activity 7.4
Crossword Puzzle—Communication

Directions

Complete the following statements and then use the answers to complete the crossword puzzle.

Across

2. _____ is any sound that interferes with clear reception during the communication process.

5. _____ is the term that refers to shortening words used while text messaging.

9. In writing, the _____ is the statement that gets readers' attention.

10. _____ is a technique used to reinforce and improve performance on the job.

11. _____ is technical language specific to a business or industry.

12. The _____ is the person who begins the communication process.

13. A _____ is something that interferes with the communication process.

Down

1. _____ communication takes place between two or more people.

3. _____ is the act of identifying with the feelings, thoughts, and attitudes of another person.

4. _____ are what words mean.

6. The _____ is the person who receives the information in the communication process.

7. _____ is the ability to focus on what another person is saying and to be able to summarize their comments.

8. _____ communication includes gestures, expressions, and other elements that are not spoken.

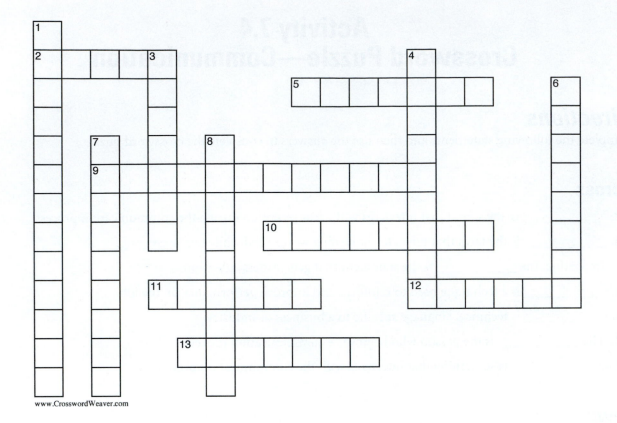

www.CrosswordWeaver.com

Activity 7.5
Active Listening

Directions

This activity will test your ability to listen and remember information. Your teacher will give a set of instructions to the first person in each line, who will repeat these instructions to the next person in line. The second person will then relay the information to the third person until everyone in the group has received the instructions. At the end of the activity, the last person in each group will repeat the instructions they received to the line leader and compare results.

Write your response to the activity below. What did you learn about communication? Present your findings to the class.

Activity 7.6
Give a "How To" Demonstration

Directions

You have been asked to demonstrate how to make a peanut butter and jelly sandwich to a group of first graders who have never made this type of sandwich. In your presentation, be sure to answer the following questions:

- What supplies are needed
- How you make the sandwich

Your presentation should not last more than 3 minutes.

When watching your classmates' presentations, complete the following chart to rate each presentation.

Presentation	Yes	No
Explained the supplies needed		
Explained the steps in the process		
Followed proper sanitation procedures		
Instructions were clear and easy to understand		
Instructions were easy to replicate		
Presenter spoke clearly		
Presenter maintained eye contact with group members		
Presenter was able to answer questions about the process		
Other notes about the presentation:		

1. Did each presenter prepare his or her sandwich in the same way? If not, is this important?

_____

_____

_____

_____

_____

_____

_____

_____

2. Overall, were the instructions easy to understand? Could the audience members recreate the sandwich on their own?

_____

_____

_____

_____

_____

_____

_____

_____

_____

_____

3. What did you learn about communication from this activity?

_____

_____

_____

_____

_____

_____

_____

_____

_____

_____

_____

_____

_____

_____

_____

_____

Activity 7.7
Role-play—Telephone Etiquette

Directions

In this activity you will have the opportunity to be a caller and a worker. Each scenario has been designed to give you experience handling different types of calls. Some questions for you to consider about each scenario are included after the scene has been described. Before beginning the activity, review the section on telephone etiquette in Section 7.2, "Communication Skills."

Scenario 1

Roles: Host, Guest Calling to Make a Dinner Reservation

You are the host for The Gourmet Grille, an upscale steakhouse in the city. It is a busy Friday evening. You answer the phone and it is an out-of-town guest wanting to make a dinner reservation for the next evening.

1. How should the phone be answered?

_____

_____

_____

_____

_____

2. What information should you ask for?

_____

_____

_____

_____

3. What should you tell the guest?

_____

_____

_____

_____

Scenario 2

Roles: Manager, Upset Guest

You are the manager of Joe's Café. The phone rings and it is a guest calling to complain about the poor service received at dinner the evening before.

During the course of the call, the guest asks to speak to your boss.

1. How should the phone be answered?

_____

_____

_____

_____

_____

2. How do you handle an upset guest on the phone?

_____

_____

_____

_____

_____

3. What should you do if the guest wishes to speak to your boss?

_____

_____

_____

_____

_____

Scenario 3

Roles: Server, Cook

It's 6:00 a.m. and the restaurant is just about to open. A server is walking past the host stand and hears the phone ring. The server stops to answer it, and it's one of the breakfast cooks calling in sick. The server can't find the manager.

1. How should the server answer the phone?

_____

_____

_____

_____

_____

2. What information should the server get from the cook?

_____

_____

_____

_____

_____

3. Where should the server write the information?

_____

_____

_____

_____

_____

Scenario 4

Roles: Server, Guest

It's 2:00 p.m on a Wednesday afternoon. The manager is in the kitchen working with the chef on the menu for the evening. One of the servers is helping clean menus at the host stand when the phone rings. The server answers the phone but cannot answer the guest's questions. The server puts the guest on hold.

1. How should the server answer the phone?

_____

_____

_____

_____

_____

2. What information should the server get from the guest?

_____

_____

_____

_____

_____

3. What should the server do when he or she can't answer the guest's questions?

_____

_____

_____

_____

_____

4. How long should the guest be kept on hold?

_____

_____

_____

_____

_____

Activity 7.8
Project—Written Communication Thank-you Notes

Directions

You will be writing a thank-you note to someone who has helped you succeed this school year.

Step 1

Decide who you will send the note to, and then write a rough draft below. Check the draft for proper spelling, punctuation, etc. In the message, be specific in terms of how this person has helped you and what it means to you.

In order for the note to be delivered, you will also need the recipient's name and mailing address.

Step 2

Take a note card and write your message.

Step 3

Address the envelope to the recipient.

Step 4

Give the completed note card and envelope to your teacher.

_____

_____

_____

_____

_____

_____

_____

_____

_____

_____

_____

_____

_____

Activity 7.9
Clarifying Written Communication

Directions

You are the owner of a restaurant where customers have recently had several negative service experiences. At your request, the assistant manager has written some follow-up letters to send to these unsatisfied customers, apologizing and encouraging them to return to the restaurant for a chance to "make it up to them."

For each of the scenarios below, improve the assistant manager's written message so that the tone is more professional and customer focused. Follow the guidelines outlined in Section 7.2, "Communication Skills, Effective Writing."

Scenario One

A family of 10 was celebrating their grandmother's 75th birthday on a busy Friday night. The service was very slow, as their server was new. Also, most of their food was served ice-cold. When one of the customers brought the problems to the attention of the assistant manager, he told the hostess to put the dinners in the microwave to warm them up, since the hostess wasn't very busy. The customer then completed a customer comment card detailing his family's disappointing experience

"All of us here at the restaurant are very sorry about the so-called misunderstanding that happened to you last week. We tried the best we could to fix the problem, once you finally told us about it. A lot of our staff has quit recently, and so we have a lot of new servers. We hope you come back to our restaurant sometime anyway. Next time, you should let us know that it is a special occasion so we are ready."

Rewrite the message below.

_____

_____

_____

_____

_____

_____

_____

_____

_____

_____

_____

Scenario Two

A group of professionals held a business lunch at your restaurant. At the beginning of the meal, the server spilled a bowl of soup on two people wearing expensive suits. The server was embarrassed and too nervous to continue serving the group. Because of that, the server avoided going to the table as much as possible—sending other servers to pick up used dishes and deliver the check. Upon paying the bill, the host of the group told the assistant manager that she was afraid the clients' suits had been ruined, and this had been a very important business opportunity for her.

"We are sorry about the spilled soup. If the server would have told the manager right away, we could have brought out some towels and water to help clean up. Here is a recommendation for a dry cleaner that is right down the block from the restaurant. Good luck with your business—give us another try sometime."

Rewrite the message below.

_____

_____

_____

_____

_____

_____

_____

_____

_____

_____

_____

Activity 7.10
Essay—Speaking the Same Language

Directions

You have been invited to apply to enter an essay that will be called "The Importance of Speaking Plainly in the Workplace." The winner of the essay contest will receive a $500 scholarship, and the winning essay will be printed in the local paper and online. The essay should be 500 words and needs to address what happens when employees and managers don't "speak the same language" in the workplace.

The contest owners would like students to focus on the problems that happen when acronyms and abbreviations are used instead of using common words. The first step in preparing for the essay is to be sure you are clear on the meaning of common business and text/chat abbreviations or lingo. If you do not know the meaning of a term, research it by looking it up online, asking a teacher, or comparing meanings with classmates.

Part 1

Acronymn/Abbreviation	Common Meaning
LOL	Laugh out loud
"86"	The kitchen has run out of an item; don't take any more orders
OMG	Oh my goodness (or similar word)
Covers	The number of guests served in a restaurant
BRB	Be right back (or bathroom break)
P&L	Profit and Loss statement
PIR	Parent in room
BOGO	Buy One Get One (free implied)
L8R	Later
2MI or TMI	Too much information
411	Information

Part 2

Write a 500-word essay explaining why it is important to speak the "same language" in order to prevent miscommunications or mishaps in the workplace. In the essay, be sure to include at least three to four words from the abbreviation list. These can be used in a story that helps make your point or as a way to be sure the reader understands your point.

Use the space provided below to write your essay or submit it as a computer-generated document.

_____

_____

_____

_____

Chapter **8**

Activity 8.1
Test Your Management IQ

Directions

Mark each of the following statements related to management as either true (T) or false (F). For each false statement, rewrite it to make it a true statement.

Part 1—Learning to Work Together

_____ 1. Diversity is a reflection of a stagnant marketplace.

_____

_____

_____ 2. Beyond fulfilling legal obligations, a diverse workplace offers many other benefits as well.

_____

_____

_____ 3. Harassment happens when slurs or other conduct related to a person's race, gender, color, sexual orientation, etc., interferes with a person's work performance or creates a hostile work environment.

_____

_____

_____ 4. Harassment only applies to sexual harassment.

_____

_____

_____ 5. By definition, a team is a group of people with diverse skills and backgrounds who come together to complete a task or common goal.

_____

_____

_____ 6. Some of the disadvantages of teamwork are allowing team members to learn from each other and allowing team members to support each other during the process.

_____

_____

Part 2—Being a Successful Leader

_____ 1. Leaders are able to inspire and motivate employees to accomplish an organization's goals.

_____

_____

_____ 2. Technical skills, such as running a machine, are known as interpersonal skills.

_____

_____

_____ 3. An example of internal motivation is a paycheck.

_____

_____

_____ 4. When the problem-solving process is followed correctly, problems will be permanently fixed.

_____

_____

_____ 5. Professional development is an ongoing process of continuous learning to help employees meet their personal or professional goals.

_____

_____

_____ 6. Ethics are guiding principles that only need to be employed when you might be caught doing something wrong.

_____

_____

_____ 7. SMART goals provide clear expectations for everyone in the workplace.

_____

_____

Part 3—Interviewing and Orientation

_____ 1. A job description is a document that describes the work and duties of a particular position.

_____

_____

_____ 2. Employees in exempt positions are guaranteed overtime pay, according to the law.

_____

_____

_____ 3. When interviewing prospective employees, the interviewer should ask about their age, religion, marital status, and disabilities.

_____

_____

_____ 4. Standardized tools, such as the job application, are used to make sure all applicants are treated fairly.

_____

_____

_____ 5. A zero tolerance policy in the workplace means that no violation is forgiven.

_____

_____

_____ 6. Onboarding is a process used by companies to integrate employees into the organization.

_____

_____

_____ 7. Orientation should be short and designed for employees to fill out any human resources paperwork.

_____

_____

Part 4—Training and Evaluation

_____ 1. Training is designed to improve the skills, knowledge, and attitudes of employees.

_____

_____

_____ 2. Cross-training is designed to teach employees how to do more than one job.

_____

_____

_____ 3. On-the-job training is an ineffective method for learning a new skill.

_____

_____

_____ 4. An employee performance appraisal is an informal review of a person's work at the end of each shift.

_____

_____

_____ 5. A self-evaluation form is a tool that allows employees and managers to set performance goals together.

_____

_____

Activity 8.2
Commercial—The Benefits of the
Multicultural Workplace

Directions

Create a 20-second radio commercial to promote the benefits of the multicultural workplace. You will need to write a script and practice the commercial to make sure that the spot is exactly 20 seconds. Your commercial should incorporate at least three of the ideas about diversity in the workplace found in Section 8.1 of your text. Your commercial may also include some type of music or sound effects. Be creative and accurate.

Take the notes for your script in the space below. Present your commercial to the class. If a tape recorder is available, record your commercial.

Activity 8.3
Poster/Presentation—Preventing Harassment
in the Workplace

Directions

You have been hired by the local EEOC office to create a series of posters designed to educate teenage workers on the different types of harassment that might occur in the workplace and steps that the worker may take to prevent or report harassment. The EEOC has explained that many younger workers are intimidated by older workers and do not report possible harassment problems.

You may choose from one of the following topics:

- Sexual
- Ethnic
- Age
- Religion
- Physical limitations

Part 1—Design a Poster

Working with your team, choose a harassment topic from the list above and design a poster to meet the scenario presented above.

Refer to *Chapter 8: Management Essentials* in your textbook for more information related to the topic. You may also choose to use the Internet for additional resources.

You may use the space provided on the next page to draw your final poster or as a practice space if you are creating your final poster with some other medium (poster board, computer, etc.).

Part 2—Develop and Deliver a Presentation

Design your presentation to address the following questions:

1. What topic did your team choose?

_____

_____

_____

_____

2. Why did your team choose this topic?

_____

_____

_____

_____

3. How did your team research the topic?

_____

_____

_____

_____

4. Why is this topic important for teen workers to understand?

_____

_____

_____

_____

5. What is your team's poster trying to convey about this topic?

_____

_____

_____

_____

_____

Activity 8.4
Teamwork and Communication

Directions

You will be working in teams to plan a small, catered dinner meeting for 20 members of the business community who are visiting local establishments in preparation for hosting their annual meeting of 200 members. The business guests will be looking for creativity and affordability.

In order to successfully complete the task you will need to stay within budget, design a 3-course meal that retails for not more than $15 per person, determine room decorations, write a description of each dish on the menu, and complete the task within 30 minutes. If you go over budget or don't complete the menu, you will be disqualified.

Item	Cost	Serving size
Entrées		
Fish (salmon filet)	$10.99/lb	6 oz
Chicken breast (boneless)	$ 7.99/lb	6 oz
Steak (sirloin)	$ 6.99/lb	4 oz
Side dishes		
Rice (long grain)	$ 0.07/oz	3 oz
Pasta (dry)	$0.11/oz.	3 oz
Potato (baked)	$0.80/lb	each
Vegetables		
Green beans (frozen)	$0.25/oz	4 oz
Carrots	$0.99/lb	4 oz
Cauliflower	$3.99/head	4 oz
Broccoli	$1.29/head	4 oz
Desserts		
Cheesecake	$7.99/7-in cake (12 slices/cake)	1 slice
Cookies (bake and scoop)	$9.99/40 oz. tub	1 cookie (1 oz.)
Ice cream (vanilla)	$2.50/½ gal	½ cup
Beverages		
Soda	$0.50/can	1 can per guest
Coffee, tea, decaf	$0.75/serving	Unlimited refills, includes condiments
Condiments		
Sauces, spices, etc.	$3.00 per person	
Decorations		
Napkins	$0.25/each	1 per guest
Centerpiece	$2.00/Each	1 per table

Take your notes in the space below. Attach your menu to this sheet.

Activity 8.5
Case Study—Problem Solving

Directions

Read the case study below. As you read, think about what you have learned about teamwork and problem solving. Then, answer the questions at the end of each case study section. Be prepared to share your answers with your classmates.

Part 1—Case Study

Casey supervises the afternoon kitchen staff at the Tiki Hut restaurant. Lately, his staff does not seem to be working as efficiently as usual. He decides to brainstorm with his employees to find out why. Opening the meeting, Casey says, "I want you to help me list the problems in our area. Let's see how many problems we can list in 10 minutes. Don't tell me how you think we ought to solve the problems or comment on what other people say. Just focus on making a list. Everything you say in this meeting will be kept confidential, so please say what you really think. Who wants to start?"

Shari says, "Ever since the Tiki Hut expanded, we've had so much more business, but we're constantly running out of supplies. I'm tired of always having to search for what I need when I'm in a hurry."

George says, "The kitchen printer is always causing problems. It either runs out of ink or the paper jams or both!"

"The storeroom is a mess," states Marcus. "It's cluttered with half-open boxes and nothing is labeled so it's hard to find anything when you need it."

Casey notices that Jen hasn't said anything. "How about you, Jen?" he asks. "What have you noticed?"

"Well, um," Jen says, "some of the servers have a habit of picking up orders that aren't theirs. They don't even bother to look at the tickets before they take the food."

"These are all great observations," says Casey. "Anything else?"

Casey has put together this list of problems from the brainstorming session with his staff in the order in which they were mentioned:

- Shortage of supplies
- Faulty kitchen printer
- Disorganized storeroom
- Servers taking the wrong orders

Case Study Questions

1. As you read the Tiki Hut case study, you may have noticed that Casey set down some ground rules for the brainstorming session. Underline places in the scene where Casey followed the ground rules listed below:

   A. Set a time limit on the brainstorming session

   B. Don't let the conversation get sidetracked

   C. Be sure everyone speaks openly

   D. Be sure everyone contributes

   E. Let those directly involved in the situation being discussed do the talking

2. Consider the events that occurred throughout the case study. In your opinion, were there any situations that could have been avoided if one of the key players had chosen different actions? If so, which ones and what might the outcome have been if they had made a different choice?

Part 2—Case Study

Casey has called another meeting with his problem-solving team. "Let's look at the problem of servers picking up the wrong orders. What do you think we could do to solve the problem?" he asks.

Shari says, "The servers don't even bother to look for a ticket when they pick up the food. Let's put up a sign reminding them."

"I don't think a sign will make a difference," Jen says. "The servers are in too much of a hurry, and they don't want to take the time to look at tickets. Why would they look at a sign?"

"They don't want to take the time," George says, "because half the time we don't get the second printout from the printer. We need to get a printer that works!"

"Even when they do print out, the fans blow the tickets around and servers can't tell which plate they belong to. If we get a new printer, let's get one that prints on heavier paper," says Rafael.

"Hmmmm," Casey says. "Sounds like you are all telling me our problem is really a combination of server habits, printer problems, and the fan. Besides server frustration, what other problems are caused?"

"Well," Jen says, "customers get upset when they aren't getting served promptly or when they receive wrong orders."

"And then," George says, "we end up remaking the food that wasn't properly delivered."

"So, it appears we have two solutions," says Casey. "Either put up a sign for the servers or buy a new printer. Any other suggestions?"

"We could hire someone as an expediter who could be sure each server takes the right orders out, " says Shari.

"I don't think we have the budget to hire another kitchen employee right now, " says Casey.

"I like George's idea of getting a new printer, although I don't think we need heavier paper. We should put the edge of the ticket under the plate," Jen says. "But buying a printer will cost money too."

"Constantly remaking orders will cost more than that in the long run, " says George.

Case Study Questions

1. In this scene, Casey followed these steps in his problem-solving meeting:

   A. Get input from everybody; clarify the problem if necessary

   B. Examine the problem's effects on employees

   C. State the specific results you want to get from a solution to the problem

   D. Brainstorm possible solutions to the problem

   Review the scene and underline the sections in which Casey used the four steps listed above.

2. Consider the events that occurred throughout the case study. In your opinion, was there anything Casey could have done differently? How would you have handled the problem-solving meeting?

_____

_____

_____

_____

_____

_____

_____

_____

_____

_____

_____

_____

_____

_____

_____

_____

_____

_____

_____

_____

Activity 8.6
Setting SMART Goals

Directions

Using the SMART goal process, write three SMART goals for something you would like to achieve in school, sports, or on the job. Fill in the worksheet with information for each category.

Specific:

_____

_____

_____

Measurable:

_____

_____

_____

Achievable:

_____

_____

_____

Relevant:

_____

_____

_____

Timebound:

_____

_____

_____

Activity 8.7
Writing a Résumé

Directions

Using the sample résumé format below, fill in the spaces provided with information about you. Think about the qualifications and experiences you have and how they relate to the job that you want. Refer to the sample résumé below for help.

Sample Résumé

Max Lippman

1234 Main Street

Anywhere, USA 12345

Phone: 555-456-7890

Objective: Server, part-time

Qualifications:

- Can use a computer
- Received high grades in foodservice classes
- Know how to organize work
- Work well with others
- Supervised others in a student kitchen

Work Experience:

2009–Present, Server Assistant, First Class Café, Anywhere, USA

Responsibilities Include:

- Clear tables quickly and correctly
- Refill water and other beverages as needed
- Assist servers in serving food
- Received "Employee of the Month"

Other Experience:

- Helped serve food at high school café as part of foodservice class
- Organized annual junior class bake sale
- Developed a new recipe for low-fat brownies sold at bake sales
- Used recipe software to type recipes for class cookbook
- Volunteered in the kitchen at a community Thanksgiving dinner

Education:

- Currently enrolled at Anywhere Community High School
- Taking food and beverage management classes

Using the sample résumé format, fill in the blanks with the information about you. Think about the qualifications and experiences you have and how they relate to the job you want. Refer to the textbook or Internet for samples.

Name:

_____

Address:

_____

City/State/Zip:

_____

Phone:

_____

Email:

_____

Objective:

_____

_____

_____

Qualifications:

_____

_____

_____

_____

_____

_____

_____

Experience:

_____

_____

_____

_____

_____

_____

_____

_____

Education:

_____

_____

_____

_____

_____

_____

_____

_____

Activity 8.8
Practice—Going for the Interview

Directions

Review the sample interview questions below. Create a few of your own interview questions as well. Then, write down what you think would be a good response to each question.

Sample Interview Questions

1. How do you enjoy your present job? Tell me a little about what you do there.

2. What do you like best/least about your job?

3. What kinds of situations do you find frustrating at work/school? Why?

4. Why do you think you would be a good employee?

5. If you could be any animal, what would you be and why?

6. How do you deal with difficult people? Give an example.

7. What do you consider to be your greatest accomplishment?

8. Give an example of a time when you worked as part of a team.

9. When you have many things to be done, how do you set priorities?

10. What would you like to be doing a year from now? Five years from now?

11. What do you expect from your supervisor? Your coworkers?

12. What is one obstacle you have overcome at school or work? How has that changed your life?

Take your notes in the space below. Attach additional pages as necessary. Present your findings to the class.

_____

_____

_____

_____

_____

_____

_____

_____

_____

_____

Activity 8.9
Demonstration—On-the-Job Training

Directions

In this activity you will have the opportunity to be the trainer and the trainee. Select one of the common restaurant activities from the list below, and prepare a three to four minute training that follows the four steps of on-the-job training. Your effectiveness as a trainer will be based on how well your trainee can perform the new task.

- Setting the table
- Answering the restaurant's telephone
- Taking a guest's order
- Taking payment from a guest
- Sharpening a knife
- Making coffee
- Cleaning a table
- Folding a napkin
- Dicing an onion

Part 1

Prepare for the training. List the steps that must be taken to complete the task. Gather any supplies that might be needed for the demonstration. Take your notes in the space below.

_____

_____

_____

_____

_____

_____

_____

_____

_____

_____

_____

_____

_____

Part 2

Tell the trainee what he or she is going to learn and demonstrate as needed.

Part 3

Let the trainee practice the task and provide constructive feedback as needed.

Use the following checklist to help you note which elements of the task the trainee performed well and which might need some additional training.

Task	Yes	Needs Improvement	Comments
Listened to instructions			
Was able to list steps in the process			
Was able to duplicate the task			
Followed safety procedures where applicable			
Other			

Part 4

Confirm that the trainee can perform the task.

Review the trainee's performance with him or her. Use the checklist from Part 3 as a guide. When discussing the trainee's performance, be sure to ask the following questions:

1. Was anything in the demonstration unclear to you?

_____

_____

_____

_____

_____

_____

_____

2. Did you feel you received enough information to perform the task successfully?

_____

_____

_____

_____

_____

_____

_____

_____

3. What additional training do you feel you need?

_____

_____

_____

_____

_____

_____

_____

_____

Activity 8.10
Crossword Puzzle—Management Essentials

Directions

Complete the following statements and then use the answers to complete the crossword puzzle.

Across

1. A _____ is a generalization made about individuals from a particular group.

3. _____ is a general attitude towards a person or group made on judgments that may have nothing to do with the abilities of the person or group.

4. _____ is the reason why a person takes action or behaves in a certain way.

6. _____-_____ happens when employees learn the functions of another job within the operation.

9. _____ involves using each members strengths so the group has more success working together.

10. _____ is a technique used to demonstrate behaviors that management would like to see.

12. _____ includes a great variety of people from a wide variety of backgrounds.

14. _____ is the ability to inspire and motivate employees.

15. _____ are statements of desired results.

16. _____ may be in the form of slurs or other abuse that interferes with an employee's ability to work.

Down

2. An _____ position is not legally entitled to receive overtime.

5. _____ is the combination of skills, knowledge, attitudes, and behaviors a person shows while performing a job.

7. _____ is the process that helps new employees learn about the policies of the company and their coworkers.

8. When materials are presented in a variety of languages, this is called _____.

11. _____ is the process a company uses to integrate new employees into the organization.

13. _____ are the set of moral values that a society holds.

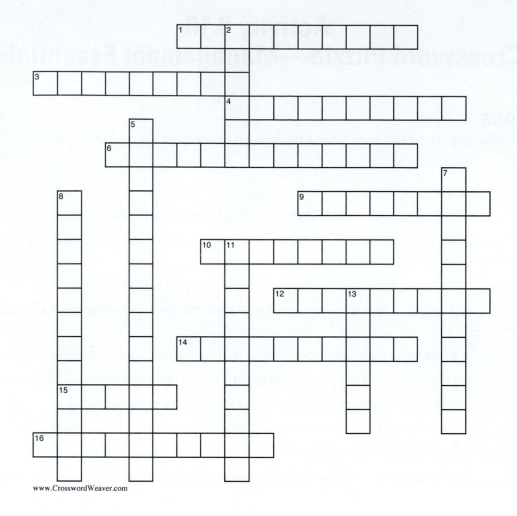

www.CrosswordWeaver.com

Chapter **9**

Activity 9.1
Test Your Knowledge of Fruits and Vegetables IQ

Directions

Mark each of the following statements related to fruits and vegetables as either true (T) or false (F). For each false statement, rewrite it to make it a true statement.

Part 1—Fruits

_____ 1. From a scientific standpoint, a fruit is an organ that develops from the ovary of a flowering plant and contains one or more seeds.

_____

_____

_____ 2. From a culinary point of view, a fruit can only be used for dessert or breakfast.

_____

_____

_____ 3. The sweetness of fruit comes from sucrose, a natural form of sugar.

_____

_____

_____ 4. A drupe is a fruit that has a central pit enclosing a single seed.

_____

_____

_____ 5. Tropical fruits are named for the climate they grow in and cannot tolerate frost.

_____

_____

_____ 6. All fruits are available year-round and provide the same high quality.

_____

_____

_____ 7. Quality grades are given to fruit by the USDA and rate a variety of factors such as size, color, shape, and texture.

_____

_____

_____ 8. Methane gas is emitted by certain fruits and helps in the ripening process.

_____

_____

_____ 9. Peeling, seeding, and trimming are all part of the fresh fruit preparation process.

_____

_____

_____ 10. Enzymatic browning happens when oxygen comes in contact with the flesh of fresh-cut fruits.

_____

_____

_____ 11. Acids help fruit break down more quickly while alkalis help them maintain their structure.

_____

_____

_____ 12. A coulis is a fruit sauce made from puréed fruits or vegetables.

_____

_____

Part 2—Vegetables

_____ 1. A vegetable is an edible herb-like plant.

_____

_____

_____ 2. Fruit vegetables are technically fruits since they come from flowering plants and have seeds.

_____

_____

_____ 3. Raw tomatoes are as rich in lycopene as cooked tomatoes.

_____

_____

_____ 4. Green leafy vegetables are very low in vitamins and minerals.

_____

_____

_____ 5. Root vegetables and tubers are related because some or all of them grow underground.

_____

_____

_____ 6. Mushrooms are part of the fungi family and never pose a risk to diners.

_____

_____

_____ 7. Hydroponic farms are used to grow vegetables indoors using nutrient-enriched water and regulated temperatures and lights.

_____

_____

_____ 8. Most vegetables should be stored in a cool, dry place.

_____

_____

_____ 9. If fresh vegetables will be peeled before using, there is no need to wash them first.

_____

_____

_____ 10. Organic foods are grown using methods that do not require the use of chemicals.

_____

_____

_____ 11. Glazing is a finishing technique used to give vegetables a glossy appearance.

_____

_____

_____ 12. The *sous vide* method of cooking uses airtight plastic bags placed in hot water and precisely controlled temperatures.

_____

_____

Activity 9.2
Report/Presentation—Fruits of the World

Directions

Research fruits from around the world. In your report include answers to the following questions:

1. Which fruit did you select? Why?

2. Describe the fruit—look, texture, and taste.

3. Which part of the world does the fruit come from?

4. Are there any special uses or stories about this fruit?

5. Include two recipes that are made from this fruit.

Use the space below to take your notes. Attach additional pages as necessary.

_____

_____

_____

_____

_____

_____

_____

_____

_____

_____

_____

_____

_____

_____

_____

_____

_____

_____

_____

Activity 9.3
Lab—Simple Fruit and Vegetable Garnishes

Directions

Garnishes are used to provide a finishing touch to a plate, buffet, or display. Learning how to create simple garnishes can provide a special touch to an everyday meal or gourmet event. Creating garnishes is a good way to become comfortable working with a variety of fruits and vegetables.

Recipe Selection

- Citrus Rose Garnish
- Strawberry Fan
- Carrot Curls
- Pineapple Boat
- Green Onion Fan

Objectives

After completing this lab activity, you should be able to:

- Apply effective *mise en place* through practice
- Demonstrate proper use of equipment and tools
- Follow basic food safety and sanitation guidelines
- Follow basic safety guidelines to avoid causing injury to self or others

Directions

1. Review the garnishes that you have been assigned.
2. Perform *mise en place*. Plan for any substitutions or additional instructions you may receive.
3. Prepare the garnish.
4. Clean up the area.

Citrus Rose Garnish

1 lemon (can also use a lemon or small orange)
1 sharp utility or paring knife

Start at the top of the lemon cutting the yellow rind (skin) only. Be sure not to include any of the white membrane. Cut one continuous strip; it is okay to make the cuts a little jagged while peeling.

Coil the strip in a circle, skin side out. Turn the coil over and put it on the plate or use for decoration.

Strawberry Fan

1 medium strawberry
1 sharp paring knife

Select a medium-sized strawberry with no noticeable blemishes or decay. Wash and dry the strawberry thoroughly. Place the strawberry on a cutting board and use the paring knife to make a series of thin slices lengthwise through the strawberry (generally 4 to 5 slices will be enough). Be sure to leave the slices attached to the hull of the strawberry. Gently fan the slices apart. Place on a plate or on top of a chilled fruit soup for garnish.

Carrot Curls

1 large carrot, washed and dry
1 vegetable peeler
1 paring knife
Toothpicks
Bowl of ice water

Select a large carrot and wash and dry thoroughly. Cut off the top and end of the carrot using a paring knife and the cutting board. Use the vegetable peeler to cut thin strips from the carrot. Note: The strips should be the length of the carrot.

Roll the thin carrot strips into curls and secure both ends with a toothpick. Put the carrot curls in a bowl of ice water to chill. Remove from water and drain before using. Remove toothpick and place garnish where needed.

Pineapple Boat

1 pineapple
1 utility knife

Cut a pineapple in half lengthwise through the crown. Carefully remove the fruit from the shell; use care when removing the fruit. Remove the core from the fruit and discard the core. Chop the remaining pineapple into chunks and place them in the pineapple half. Add additional fruit, such as melon balls, strawberries, etc. Note: This can be used to garnish a presentation or to serve a variety of salads.

Green Onion Fan

1 green onion or scallion
1 paring knife
Ice water
Plastic twist tie

Wash and dry the green onion thoroughly. Place green onion on the cutting board and cut off the root end. Throw this away. Begin cutting about 1 inch from the green part of the onion, making several lengthwise cuts in the white part near the root end. These cuts should be close together. Leave about 1 inch of green above the white root; cut and discard the rest of the green.

Use a rubber band or twist tie to hold the uncut green parts together. Place the onion in ice water until ready to use. Watch the cut portions fan out. Remove the rubber band or twist tie before serving.

Activity 9.4
Demonstration or Field Trip—Purchasing Fresh Produce

Directions

In this activity you will learn how to select fresh fruit and/or vegetables. From the produce available, choose one item that is in excellent condition and one that is less than optimal. Explain to the class what makes a good piece of produce and what are the signs of a bad or servable piece of produce.

While discussing fresh produce and possibly spoiled produce, include the following:

■ Color

■ Texture

■ Smell

■ Blemishes/Bruising

■ Location (where did the produce come from)

Use the space below to take your notes. Present your findings to the class.

_____

_____

_____

_____

_____

_____

_____

_____

_____

_____

_____

_____

_____

_____

_____

_____

_____

Activity 9.5
Lab—Cooking with Fruit

Directions

Fruits can be used in a variety of methods, from a cold fruit salad to a refreshing dessert or a sauce used to enhance an entrée. There are also many cooking methods that can be used when working with fruit. As you have discovered, fruit can be prepared in many ways to enhance its flavor, texture, color, and nutrients.

Recipe Selection

- Tropical Fruit Salad
- Applesauce
- Orange-Blueberry-Banana Smoothie
- Broiled Pineapple

Objectives

After completing this lab activity, you should be able to:

- Apply effective *mise en place* through practice
- Demonstrate proper use of equipment and tools
- Follow basic food safety and sanitation guidelines
- Follow basic safety guidelines to avoid causing injury to self or others
- Match and cook fruits to appropriate methods

Directions

1. Review the recipe you have been assigned.
2. Perform *mise en place*. Plan for any substitutions or additional instructions you have been given.
3. Prepare the recipe.
4. Clean up the area.

Tropical Fruit Salad

Yield: 10 servings

Measure	Ingredients
6 oz (1 cup)	Mango, diced
6 oz (1 cup)	Pineapple, diced
6 oz (1 cup)	Melon, diced (or melon balls)
6 oz (1 cup)	Papaya, diced
3 fl oz	Orange juice
6 oz (1 cup)	Bananas, sliced
2 oz (¾ cup)	Coconut, shredded, unsweetened

Directions

1. Toss the mango, pineapple, melon, and papaya together with the orange juice.

2. Keep chilled until service time.

3. Arrange the fruit salad on chilled plates and top with bananas. Top with coconut and serve at once.

4. Optional presentation: Use a hollowed-out pineapple boat instead of a chilled plate.

Applesauce

Yield: 4 cups

Measure	Ingredients
3 lb (9½ cups)	Apples, peeled, cored, and sliced
4 fl oz	Apple juice or water
2 Tbsp	Sugar (plus more as needed)
⅛ tsp	Salt
1 tsp	Cinnamon, ground (optional)

Directions

1. Combine the apples, apple juice or water, sugar, and salt in a heavy gauge saucepan.

2. Simmer over low heat until the apples are tender and starting to fall apart, about 10 minutes.

3. Purée the apples and any liquid in the pan by pushing them through a food mill or puréeing in a food processor.

4. Taste and adjust the seasoning with cinnamon (if using) or additional sugar.

5. Serve warm or cool.

Broiled Pineapple

Yield: 8

Measure	Ingredients
1 each	Pineapple, fresh (about 3½ to 4 lb), trimmed, cored, and sliced in half lengthwise
1½ tbsp	Dark brown sugar, packed
1 cup	Pineapple juice
½ cup	Coconut, shredded

Directions

1. Preheat broiler.

2. Slice halves of pineapple into halves. You will have 4 slices.

3. Line a 1-quart shallow baking dish with foil.

4. Combine the brown sugar and pineapple juice in a small bowl.

5. Stir the ingredients until the sugar is dissolved.

6. Arrange the pineapple slices in a single layer in the baking dish.

7. Drizzle evenly with the juice mixture.

8. Broil the pineapple 5 inches from the heat until the slices are lightly browned, about 5 to 8 minutes.

9. Sprinkle with the coconut.

10. Continue broiling until the coconut is lightly browned, about 3 to 4 minutes.

11. Plate and drizzle the pineapple slices with the remaining juices.

12. Serve immediately.

Orange-Blueberry-Banana Smoothie

Yield: 2 cups

Measure	Ingredients
1 cup	Vanilla low-fat yogurt
1 cup	Blueberries, washed and patted dry
½	Banana, peeled
½ cup	Orange juice
½ cup	Ice

Directions

1. Combine all ingredients in a blender.
2. Process on high speed until smooth.
3. Serve immediately.

Activity 9.6
Editorial—The Importance of Fresh Fruits and Vegetables

Directions

Write an editorial about the importance of fresh fruits and vegetables in the daily diet. Find statistics on the Internet about the importance of fresh fruits and vegetables in maintaining good health. Use the material in *Chapter 9: Fruits and Vegetables* as a starting point.

Use the space below to take your notes. Attach additional pages as necessary. Present your findings to the class.

_____

_____

_____

_____

_____

_____

_____

_____

_____

_____

_____

_____

_____

_____

_____

_____

_____

_____

_____

_____

_____

_____

Activity 9.7
Lab—Vegetable Cookery

Directions

Vegetables lend themselves to an unlimited variety of cooking methods—from boiling to blanching, to steaming and roasting. As you have learned, vegetables should be prepared in ways that best retain their unique textures, flavors, colors, and nutrients.

Recipe Selection

- Baked Acorn Squash with Cranberry-Orange Compote
- Broccoli Mousse
- Eggplant Parmesan
- Green Beans with Bacon, Shallots, and Mushrooms
- Green Beans with Tomatoes
- Grilled Vegetables
- Roasted Vegetables

Objectives

After completing this lab activity, you should be able to:

- Apply effective *mise en place* through practice
- Demonstrate proper use of equipment and tools
- Follow basic food safety and sanitation guidelines
- Follow basic safety guidelines to avoid causing injury to self or others
- Identify, describe, and demonstrate the preparation of different types of vegetables
- Match and cook vegetables to appropriate methods

Directions

1. Review the recipes you have been assigned.
2. Perform *mise en place.* Plan for any substitutions or additional instructions you have been given.
3. Prepare the recipe.
4. Clean up the area.

Baked Acorn Squash with Cranberry-Orange Compote

Yield: 8 servings

Measure	Ingredients
6 oz	Butter, melted
4 oz	Brown sugar, honey, or maple syrup
3 small	Acorn squashes, seeds removed and cut into quarters
To taste	Salt
To taste	Pepper
Compote	
1 lb	Cranberries
6 oz	Orange juice
As needed	Chicken stock
As needed	Sugar
2 oz	Orange zest, blanched

Directions

1. Combine butter and brown sugar, honey, or maple syrup.

2. Season squash with salt and pepper, and brush with glaze. Reserve extra glaze.

3. Bake squash at 375°F for 30 minutes (cooking time varies with size of squash). Baste periodically with reserved glaze.

4. To make compote, combine cranberries, orange juice, and enough stock to barely cover cranberries. Add sugar to taste.

5. Simmer over medium heat until cranberries are softened and thick. Add orange zest.

6. At service time, spoon hot cranberry compote over squash.

© Michael Zema, FMP/CCE. Used with permission.

Broccoli Mousse

Yield: 10 Servings

Measure	Ingredients
1 lb	Broccoli, cooked until tender and puréed
4	Whole eggs
1	Egg yolk
2 to 3 oz	Heavy cream
As needed	Cream cheese, softened
To taste	Salt
To taste	White pepper

Directions

1. Combine all ingredients until smooth.

2. Fill buttered 2-ounce timbales with mixture. Arrange timbales in water bath and cover with buttered parchment paper.

3. Bake until skewer inserted in center of timbale comes out clean.

4. Remove timbales from water bath and keep warm. Unmold and serve mousse with choice of sauce or coulis.

Variations

Red Pepper Mousse
Substitute broccoli with puréed roasted red peppers.

Beet Mousse
Substitute broccoli with puréed cooked beets. Flavor with orange zest and small amount of orange juice concentrate to taste, if desired.

© Michael Zema, FMP/CCE. Used with permission.

Eggplant Parmesan

Yield: 6 servings

Measure	Ingredients
¼ cup	Cake flour
½ tsp	Salt
1 medium	Eggplant, peeled and cut into ½-inch slices
1	Egg, beaten
¼ cup	Vegetable oil
½ cup	Parmesan cheese, grated
16 oz	Tomato sauce
6 oz	Mozzarella cheese, sliced
To taste	Salt
To taste	Pepper

Directions

1. Combine flour and salt.

2. Dip eggplant slices into egg, followed by flour mixture.

3. Heat oil until hot. Brown eggplant slices in oil, about 2 to 3 minutes on each side. Drain well on paper towel.

4. Arrange half of eggplant slices in a single layer in a 10 × 6 × 2-inch pan.

5. Sprinkle half of the Parmesan cheese over eggplant slices.

6. Ladle half of the tomato sauce over the Parmesan. Sprinkle half of the mozzarella over the tomato sauce.

7. Repeat process for top layer.

8. Bake, uncovered, in a 400°F oven for 15 minutes.

Variation

Asiago cheese can be substituted for half of the Parmesan cheese portion.

© **Michael Zema, FMP/CCE. Used with permission.**

Green Beans with Bacon, Shallots, and Mushrooms

Yield: 8 servings

Measure	Ingredients
4 oz	Bacon, julienne
1 oz	Shallots, minced
2½ lb	Green beans, fresh, trimmed
8 oz	Mushrooms, fresh, sliced
To taste	Salt
To taste	Pepper

Directions

1. Sauté the bacon until partially cooked. Add shallots and cook until translucent.

2. Add green beans and sauté until al dente.

3. Add the mushrooms and cook until tender, about 2 to 3 minutes.

4. Adjust seasoning with salt and pepper.

Note

To help soften beans, add 2 ounces of white stock to the pan and cover during Step 2.

© **Michael Zema, FMP/CCE. Used with permission.**

Green Beans with Tomatoes

Yield: 8 servings

Measure	Ingredients
2 lb	Green beans, fresh, ends trimmed
6 oz	Fresh, stewed, or fire-roasted tomatoes, medium dice
2 oz	Butter, olive oil, or other fat
1 oz	Shallots, minced
1 tsp	Garlic, minced
2 tsp	Fresh basil, chopped
To taste	Salt
To taste	Pepper

Directions

1. Blanch green beans until ¾ cooked (remaining crisp and green). Shock in cold water.

2. Heat oil or fat in sauté pan. Add shallots and garlic, and sauté lightly.

3. Add beans and sauté until al dente.

4. Add tomatoes and basil and continue to sauté until tomatoes are cooked.

5. Adjust seasoning to taste with salt and pepper.

© Michael Zema, FMP/CCE. Used with permission.

Grilled Vegetables

Yield: 8 servings

Measure	Ingredients
40 oz	Assorted vegetables, according to season (leeks, fennel, sweet peppers, summer squash, etc.)
Marinade	
16 oz	Olive oil
6 oz	Soy sauce
1 tbsp	Garlic, minced
½ tsp	Fennel seeds
To taste	Lemon juice
To taste	Salt
To taste	Pepper

Directions

1. Slice vegetables into pieces thick enough to withstand the grill's heat. Precook or blanch vegetables with longer cooking times.

2. Combine all marinade ingredients.

3. Coat vegetables with marinade. Drain any excess marinade before grilling.

4. Place vegetables on hot grill. Grill both sides evenly, making crosshatch marks if desired.

© **Michael Zema, FMP/CCE. Used with permission.**

Roasted Vegetables

Yield: 6 to 8 servings

Measure	Ingredients
1 lb	Eggplant, medium dice
1 lb	Zucchini, batonnet
1 lb	Squash, medium dice
1 lb	Onion, batonnet
3	Portabella mushrooms, medium dice
2 tbsp	Butter, melted
2 tbsp	Olive oil
1 tbsp	Balsamic vinegar
1 tsp	Thyme
To taste	Salt
To taste	Pepper
1 lb	Carrots, ¼-inch slices

Directions

1. Preheat oven to 375°F.

2. Combine eggplant, zucchini, squash, onion, and mushrooms.

3. Combine butter, oil, vinegar, thyme, salt, and pepper.

4. Coat carrots with butter mixture and place in a roasting pan, roast for 15 minutes.

5. Toss remaining vegetables with butter mixture.

6. Add remaining vegetables to roasting pan and continue roasting for 15 to 20 minutes. (Roasting times might vary depending on vegetables.)

© **Michael Zema, FMP/CCE. Used with permission.**

Activity 9.8
Poster/Presentation—What's So Special About Truffles?

Directions

Research truffles used in cooking, using Internet resources, cookbooks, and culinary reference books. While conducting your research, be sure to include the following information:

- Types of truffles
  - Include pictures
  - Price of truffles
- A brief history of truffles
- Growing truffles
- Hunting for truffles
- Why truffles are valued by the modern chef
- Recipes using truffles

Create your presentation using PowerPoint or other presentation software, poster board, or a combination of visual aids.

Use the space below to take your notes. Present your findings to the class.

_____

_____

_____

_____

_____

_____

_____

_____

_____

_____

_____

_____

_____

Activity 9.9
Lab—Tubers and Root Vegetables

Directions

Tubers and root vegetables are delicious and nutritious. There are many different ways to prepare these vegetables.

Recipe Selection

- Glazed Carrots
- Ratatouille
- Sautéed Mushrooms
- Sweet Potato Chips

Objectives

After completing this lab activity, you should be able to:

- Apply effective *mise en place* through practice.
- Demonstrate proper use of equipment and tools.
- Follow basic food safety and sanitation guidelines.
- Follow basic safety guidelines to avoid causing injury to self or others.
- Identify, describe, and demonstrate the preparation of different types of vegetables.
- Match and cook vegetables to appropriate methods.

Directions

1. Review the recipes you have been assigned.
2. Perform *mise en place*. Plan for any substitutions or additional instructions you have been given.
3. Prepare the recipe.
4. Clean up the area.

Glazed Carrots

Yield: 10 Servings

Measure	Ingredients
2 oz (¼ cup)	Butter, unsalted
2½ lb (8 cups)	Carrots, oblique cut
1⅓ oz (3 tbsp)	Sugar
¼ tsp	Salt
⅛ tsp	White pepper, freshly ground
10 fl oz	Chicken or vegetable stock, hot

Directions

1. Melt the butter in a large sauté pan.
2. Add the carrots.
3. Cover the pan.
4. Lightly cook the carrots over medium-low heat for about 2 to 3 minutes.
5. Add the sugar, salt, pepper, and stock.
6. Bring the stock to a simmer.
7. Cover the pan tightly.
8. Cook over low heat until the carrots are almost tender, about 5 minutes.
9. Remove the cover.
10. Continue to simmer until the cooking liquid reduces to a glaze and the carrots are tender, about 2 to 3 minutes.
11. Adjust seasoning with salt and pepper.

Ratatouille

Yield: 10 servings

Measure	Ingredients
2 fl oz	Olive oil
12 oz (3 cups)	Onion, medium dice
¾ oz (2 tbsp)	Garlic, minced
1 oz (2 tbsp)	Tomato paste
4 oz (1 cup)	Green pepper, medium dice
14 oz (5 cups)	Eggplant, medium dice
10 oz (2 cups)	Zucchini, medium dice
5 oz (2 cups)	Mushrooms, quartered or sliced
7 oz (1 cup)	Tomato *concassé*, medium dice
6 fl oz	Chicken or vegetable stock
1 oz (¾ cup)	Herbs, fresh, chopped
To taste	Salt and black pepper, freshly ground

Directions

1. In a large pot, heat the oil over medium heat.
2. Add the onions.
3. Sauté until the onions are translucent, about 4 to 5 minutes.
4. Add the garlic.
5. Sauté until the aroma is apparent, about 1 minute.
6. Turn the heat to medium-low.
7. Add the tomato paste.
8. Cook until paste completely coats the onions and a deeper color is developed, about 1 to 2 minutes.
9. Add the vegetables. Cook each vegetable until it softens before adding the next.
10. Add the stock.
11. Turn the heat to low, allowing the vegetables to stew.
12. Stew until vegetables are tender and flavorful.
13. Adjust the seasoning with fresh herbs, salt, and pepper.
14. Serve immediately or cool and hold for later service.

Sautéed Mushrooms

Yield: 25 servings

Measure	Ingredients
6½ lb	Mushrooms, fresh
10 oz	Clarified butter or half oil/half butter
To taste	Salt
To taste	Pepper

Directions

1. Rinse mushrooms quickly, and gently dry them off using a paper towel.

2. Heat two or three sauté pans over high heat. Add the butter to the pans.

3. Gently add the mushrooms to the pan, and sauté over high heat until browned. When placing the mushrooms in the pan, be sure to leave room in the pan.

4. Be careful not to overcook or the mushrooms will shrivel.

5. Season with salt and pepper.

Sweet Potato Chips

Yield: 10 servings

Measure	Ingredients
2 lb	Sweet potatoes, peeled
To taste	Salt
To taste	Pepper

Directions

1. Using a slicer or mandoline, slice potatoes very thin.

2. Blanch potatoes in 325°F oil until tender.

3. Finish frying potatoes in 375°F oil until they are very crisp.

4. Drain well. Season with salt and pepper to taste.

5. Serve immediately.

© **Michael Zema, FMP/CCE. Used with permission.**

Activity 9.10
Research—Vegetarian Diets

Directions

Using the Internet, cookbooks, culinary references, magazines, and journals about vegetarianism, etc., research why people eat a vegetarian diet and the health benefits and/or risks of a vegetarian diet. Write a two- to three-page essay on any aspect of vegetarianism. Your essay can focus on the benefits of being a vegetarian or why you believe vegetarianism is not healthy. Be sure to cite your sources in the paper and present a compelling story.

Use the space below to take your notes. Attach additional pages as necessary. Present your findings to your class.

_____

_____

_____

_____

_____

_____

_____

_____

_____

_____

_____

_____

_____

_____

_____

_____

_____

_____

_____

_____

_____

_____

Chapter **10**

Activity 10.1
Test Your Service IQ

Directions

Mark each of the following statements related to service as either true (T) or false (F). For each false statement, rewrite it to make it a true statement.

Part I—The Importance of Customer Service

_____ 1. Hospitality is the feeling that guests take with them from their experience with the operation.

_____

_____

_____ 2. The ability to provide good service is something people are born with; it can not be improved through training.

_____

_____

_____ 3. First impressions are often the strongest impression that people have of a business, person, or place.

_____

_____

_____ 4. The appearance of a restaurant and its employees is not important to providing a positive guest experience.

_____

_____

_____ 5. Every guest who visits a restaurant has the same needs; guests should be treated the same.

_____

_____

_____ 6. Service can be measured by how well employees are performing their jobs.

_____

_____

_____ 7. Part of anticipating guest needs comes from watching and listening to the customers.

_____

_____

_____ 8. It is more important to please the manager than the customer.

_____

_____

Part 2—Ensuring a Positive Dining Experience

_____ 1. It is important to have an effective reservation process in place to ensure guest information is not lost or mishandled.

_____

_____

_____ 2. The greeter is responsible for checking to see if a guest has a reservation and noting any special requests the guest might have.

_____

_____

_____ 3. Suggestive selling can help the guest have a more enjoyable dining experience by making recommendations for items that will complement the guests' dining choices.

_____

_____

_____ 4. To be effective in suggestive selling, the server needs limited knowledge of the menu.

_____

_____

_____ 5. Servers may face criminal charges if found serving alcohol to a minor.

_____

_____

_____ 6. When accepting payment by credit card, the cashier should verify the guest signature on the credit card receipt to the signature on the credit card.

_____

_____

_____ 7. Customer comment cards are a quick way to gather information about a customer's dining experience.

_____

_____

_____ 8. When handling a guest complaint, blaming other employees or calling the guest names are effective methods for resolving the situation.

_____

_____

Part 3—Service Styles, Set-ups, and Staff

_____ 1. When serving food in the American style, all items are plated in the kitchen by cooks and brought to the table by the server.

_____

_____

_____ 2. French-style service is also known as family-style service.

_____

_____

_____ 3. Quick-serve restaurants are more contemporary, and the guest usually orders his or her food at a counter or drive-thru.

_____

_____

_____ 4. In the traditional service style, the dinner fork is used for all courses except dessert.

_____

_____

_____ 5. A bouillon spoon and a soup spoon are identical.

_____

_____

_____ 6. Hot beverages are served in thick glass or ceramic mugs or cups to help the beverage stay hot.

_____

_____

_____ 7. A monkey dish is a bowl used for serving Bananas Foster or similar dishes.

_____

_____

_____ 8. In a formal dining room, the maître d' is responsible for ensuring quality service for all dining room guests.

_____

_____

Activity 10.2
Poster/Presentation—Identifying Customers' Needs

Directions

You have been asked by the president of a local service club to give a 5-minute presentation on identifying customers needs in a restaurant. Your presentation should also include a visual component—this could be a poster, PowerPoint, or some other creative solution. Your presentation should address the following concepts:

- Why is it important to understand different needs?

- What are some ways that employees can address these needs?

- What are some ways that employees can make guests feel more comfortable if they have special/unique needs?

- How is this important to building business?

Part 1—Design Your Visuals

Working with your team, determine your key elements. Create a visual presentation that highlights the important areas of your presentation.

Refer to *Chapter 10: Serving Your Guests* for more information.

You may use the space provided below to sketch out your ideas and then complete the final presentation using poster board or some other medium, such as presentation software, etc.

Part 2—Develop and Deliver Your Presentation

Be sure your presentation addresses the concepts that the event planner requested. Time your presentation so that it does not exceed 5 minutes. Decide which team member will present which subjects. Take your notes in the space below. Present your findings to the class.

Activity 10.3
Scenarios—Service Slipups

Directions

As you read the scenarios below, think about what you have learned about providing excellent customer service. For each scenario, identify at least two service slipups for each scenario and list the steps you would take to prevent the problem from happening again.

Scenario 1

A group of customers has stood waiting at the entrance of a full-service operation for 10 minutes. Several employees have passed them, but no one has greeted or acknowledged them. Finally, the hostess comes out of the kitchen, hands another customer several paper bags, and without apology, seats the group.

Service Slipup 1:

_____

_____

Steps I would take to correct this from happening again:

_____

_____

_____

_____

_____

Service Slipup 2:

_____

_____

Steps I would take to correct this from happening again:

_____

_____

_____

_____

_____

Scenario 2

A woman has ordered a sandwich and drink from a quick-service counter. She takes it to her car, opens the bag, and finds that she has been given the wrong sandwich and wrong-sized drink. She returns to the counter, visibly annoyed, and waits for several minutes for an employee to finish with another customer before acknowledging her. When she tells the employee her problem, the employee takes the bag from her, yells at another employee for messing up the order, and hands her another bag without comment.

Service Slipup 1:

_____

_____

Steps I would take to correct this from happening again:

_____

_____

_____

_____

_____

_____

_____

Service Slipup 2:

_____

_____

Steps I would take to correct this from happening again:

_____

_____

_____

_____

_____

_____

_____

Scenario 3

As a customer walks through a cafeteria line, he stops at nearly every item and asks the nearest employee the following questions: "What's this?" "Does this have salt?" "Is this very spicy?" "Is this broiled or grilled?" The employees become visibly annoyed by his constant questions, rolling their eyes and looking at each other with smirks. One employee answers him by saying, "What do we look like, tour guides?" The man is embarrassed, sets his tray down in the middle of the line, and walks out.

Service Slipup 1:

_____

_____

Steps I would take to correct this from happening again:

_____

_____

_____

_____

_____

_____

_____

Service Slipup 2:

_____

_____

Steps I would take to correct this from happening again:

_____

_____

_____

_____

_____

_____

_____

Activity 10.4
Create a Reservation System

Directions

You have been hired by the owner of a new chain of restaurants to design a reservation system. Each restaurant in the chain seats between 100 and 150 guests. The restaurants are so popular, reservations are required for Friday and Saturday evenings. The current reservation system is not working. You will meet with the owner to find out the needs of the restaurant and then work with the owner to design a new reservation system.

Part 1—Brainstorm the Needs of the Reservation System

Brainstorm the items that must be included in order for the reservations to be taken efficiently and accurately.

Take your notes in the space below.

_____

_____

_____

_____

_____

_____

_____

_____

Part 2—Design the System

This can be a paper-and-pen system or it can be a computerized system.

Take your notes in the space below.

_____

_____

_____

_____

_____

_____

_____

Part 3—Test the System

Working with a person from another team, test the system, and make note of any feedback for improvements.

Take your notes in the space below.

_____

_____

_____

_____

_____

_____

_____

Part 4—Present the System

Present the finished system to your class.

Activity 10.5
Suggestive Selling

Directions

Below are eight sentences that have lost their "other halves." Help these sentences make sense again by connecting the phrases on the left with those that best complete them on the right. Some pairs have more than one possible answer, and answers may be used more than once.

	1. Good listening skills are essential to . . .	A. . . . leave them alone. Let them decide at their own pace, without forcing them to make a decision.
	2. Suggestive selling refers to . . .	B. . . . right from the moment the guests sit down at the table.
	3. Saying, "Would you like to try our homemade cheesecake, topped with fresh country blueberries?" is a way to . . .	C. . . . answer the guests' questions and suggest menu alternatives.
	4. Let customers know they've made a good decision ordering their food . . .	D. . . . servers' attitudes, actions, and appearances.
	5. If customers don't know what to order, or take a long time to decide, you should . . .	E. . . . suggest items using colorful descriptions and phrases.
	6. Following up with customers and saying, "good-bye" and "hello" are examples of . . .	F. . . . the role the server has in suggesting items to guests and increasing check averages.
	7. All operations are represented through their décor, theme, and menu, and also by . . .	G. . . . so they are pleased with their decision and look forward to their meal.
	8. It is a good idea to recommend promotions and specials . . .	H. . . . great ways to make guests feel eager and excited to return.

Activity 10.6
Experiential Activity—Restaurant Visit

Directions

You have been asked to be a "mystery shopper" for the owner of a group of several foodservice operations. Visit one of your favorite places to eat, and complete the following survey about your experience. To get the most accurate picture of service at the restaurant, try not to let the server see you marking down your observations. Hint: Review the checklist items before your visit so you know what you are going to be observing.

Mystery Shopper Report

Date: _____ Time: _____

Restaurant Name: _____ Location: _____

Server Name (or Description): _____

	Yes	No
1. Were you greeted in a prompt and friendly manner?		
2. Did the server/order taker make eye contact with you?		
3. Did the server/order taker listen carefully as you placed your order?		
4. Did the server/order taker repeat your order to confirm it?		
5. Was the restaurant clean?		
6. Did the cashier/order taker handle the payment in a professional manner?		
7. When you received your order was everything correct?		

8. What did the server's body language communicate to you during the time you were being helped?

_____

_____

_____

_____

_____

_____

_____

_____

9. If you had to guess if the server was happy to be helping you or not, what would you guess?

_____

_____

_____

_____

_____

_____

_____

_____

10. If there was a problem with your order (it was incorrect, took a long time, etc.) how well did the server understand and fix the problem?

_____

_____

_____

_____

_____

_____

_____

_____

_____

11. What did you learn from this experience?

_____

_____

_____

_____

_____

_____

_____

_____

Activity 10.7
Design a Comment Card

Directions

You have been asked to create a customer comment card for a local restaurant. Working together as a class, follow these steps to design a comment card:

- Step 1: Decide categories, such as questions about food and service, questions about price, etc.

- Step 2: Develop a rating system.

- Step 3: Decide if you want written comments.

- Step 4: Decide what customer contact information you need.

- Step 5: Decide on a design.

After these five items have been determined, work individually to create a physical version of the comment card. Be prepared to share this with your classmates.

Take your notes in the space below.

_____
_____
_____
_____
_____
_____
_____
_____
_____
_____
_____
_____

Activity 10.8
Case Study—Handling Customer Complaints

Directions

Read the case study below. As you read, think about what you have learned about providing excellent customer service. Then answer the questions at the end of the case study. Be prepared to discuss with your classmates.

Case Study

Rob was scheduled to work the dinner shift at Sparkman's Steak House. He was not looking forward to working. He had argued with his girlfriend earlier in the day about his decision not to attend prom. To top it off, Tuesday nights were always very slow, and he would be lucky to have two tables to serve. But, it was too late in the day to find someone to cover his shift.

When Rob arrived at the restaurant, he changed into his uniform and walked out to the restaurant floor. Joyce, the hostess, greeted Rob and told him she had just seated a party of six in his station. Rob walked slowly to the wait stand to get water for his new party. After placing six glasses of water on a tray, Rob went to greet the guests. While placing the water glasses on their table, Rob said quietly, "My name is Rob, and I'll be your server tonight. Can I bring you something to drink?"

"My husband will have an unsweetened ice tea, I'd like a diet soda, and the kids will each have milk," said one of the guests.

"I'll be right back with your drinks," said Rob. When Rob returned, he said, "Here are your drinks. Are you ready to order?"

"We would like an appetizer first. How about the crab cakes and the calamari?"

"Okay," Rob said in a disapproving tone.

"Is there a problem with our choice?" the guest asked.

"Not really," said Rob, "I just don't like squid—it's too chewy. But it's your food! You want anything else?"

"I think we need a few more minutes," replied the guest. After leaving the table, Rob wandered over to the hostess stand to talk to Joyce. "What's wrong?" Joyce asked. Rob began to explain the details of the fight with his girlfriend. Several minutes later, Matt, the server assistant, came up and said, "Rob, your table is looking for you. They're ready to order." Rob returned to the table and took the guests' dinner order, then went to check on their appetizers.

On the way to get the appetizers, Rob saw Joyce and decided to quickly finish his conversation. Afterward, he ran to get the appetizers and rushed them to the table. A few moments later he was notified that his table's dinner order was ready. He gathered the food and took it to the table. "We just got our appetizers," commented the man. Rob replied, "Yeah, the kitchen works fast sometimes," and tossed their dinner orders down on the table. "You want anything else?"

"Yes," the woman replied, "we'd like refills on our drinks."

"Sure, right away," Rob said. Rob returned quickly with their fresh drinks. As he walked away, the woman said, "Excuse me, can we please have some steak sauce?"

"Sure," Rob replied. "Be right back." Rob brought the steak sauce to the table and then returned to the wait stand.

After 15 minutes or so, Rob noticed that his guests had finished eating. He quickly wrote up their check and returned to their table to clear the dishes and deliver the check.

After his customers left, Rob was surprised to see that he had been left a very small tip and that he had received poor service ratings on his comment card.

Case Study Questions

1. List at least three things that Rob did wrong.

_____

_____

_____

_____

_____

_____

_____

_____

_____

_____

_____

_____

2. What are three things that Rob could have done to impress his customers with top-notch customer service?

_____

_____

_____

_____

_____

_____

_____

_____

_____

_____

3. If you were Rob's manager, what would you do to help him improve his customer-service skills?

_____

_____

_____

_____

_____

_____

_____

_____

_____

_____

_____

Activity 10.9
Kitchen Activity—Proper Plate Garnish and Presentation

Directions

You have been asked by the chef to create plating guides for three new menu items that will be introduced to the guests at the Peachtree Diner next month. It is important that each plate served by the kitchen has a consistent look so that guests know what to expect when they order. Working with your teammates, create a plating guide for each of the following items:

1. Breakfast

2. Lunch

3. Dinner

Each plate should include one protein (meat, fish, chicken, etc.), one starch (potato, rice, pasta), and one fruit or vegetable plus an appropriate garnish.

Part 1

Use the workplace below to write your descriptions of the plates.

Breakfast Description

_____
_____
_____
_____
_____
_____

Lunch Description

_____
_____
_____
_____
_____
_____

Dinner Description

_____

_____

_____

_____

_____

_____

Part 2

Using the descriptions you have written, create a plating guide that the cooks can use when preparing the item. The plating guide should be a diagram or picture that is labeled to show where each component of the meal should be placed on the plate.

Take your notes in the space below. Create the final guide using poster board or on the computer. Present your findings to the class.

_____

_____

_____

_____

_____

_____

_____

_____

_____

_____

_____

_____

_____

_____

_____

_____

Activity 10.10
Presentation—Table Set-up and Layout

Directions

You have been hired by a local club to cater a special event. The meeting planner for the organization expects you and your team to make a brief presentation to show the service presentations that your operation offers.

You may choose one of the following events:

- High tea for a women's social club
- Buffet luncheon for a group of high school business students
- Formal dinner for a group of business executives
- Birthday party for a 10-year-old
- Retirement party
- Family reunion

Following are the menus for the events:

High Tea

- Assorted finger sandwiches
- Assorted miniature tarts and cakes
- Assorted teas

Buffet Luncheon/Birthday Party/Family Reunion

- Assorted bread and rolls
- Grilled chicken breast
- Hamburgers with appropriate condiments
- Hot dogs with appropriate condiments
- French fries
- Tossed salad with choice of dressing
- Assorted cookies
- Assorted soft drinks

Formal Dinner/Retirement Party

- Assorted breads and rolls
- Grilled salmon
- Prime rib
- Baked potato with toppings
- Chef's choice of vegetable
- Apple pie
- Chocolate cake
- Coffee, tea, decaf

In your presentation, include the following information:

- Service style
- Table set-up
- Type of china
- Type of glassware
- Type of silverware
- Napkin fold

Create a poster, PowerPoint presentation, or report that shows each of the elements required by the meeting planner along with a brief description of why you selected the specific style of service.

Take your notes in the space below. Attach additional pages as necessary. Present your findings to the class.

_____

_____

_____

_____

_____

_____

_____

_____

_____

_____

_____

_____

Chapter **11**

Activity 11.1
Test Your Knowledge of Potatoes and Grains IQ

Directions

Mark each of the following statements related to potatoes and grains as either true (T) or false (F). For each false statement, rewrite it to make it a true statement.

Part 1—Potatoes

_____ 1. All potatoes are the same with no variation in starch or moisture content.

_____

_____

_____ 2. New potatoes are low in starch, high in moisture, and are best for boiling, steaming, and oven roasting.

_____

_____

_____ 3. When selecting potatoes, look for ones that have dark spots, green areas, or large cuts.

_____

_____

_____ 4. The maximum storage period for russet and all-purpose potatoes is 30 days.

_____

_____

_____ 5. Solanine is a harmful, bitter-tasting substance that can be found in sprouts or if a potato has been exposed to air.

_____

_____

_____ 6. There are two categories for cooking potatoes: single-stage and multiple-stage.

_____

_____

_____ 7. Potatoes are 80 percent solid and 20 percent water.

_____

_____

_____ 8. Tubers are fat, underground stems capable of growing a new plant.

_____

_____

Part 2—Legumes and Grains

_____ 1. Legumes are seeds from pod-producing plants.

_____

_____

_____ 2. Peanuts are a type of bean.

_____

_____

_____ 3. Dried beans must be used within 30 days or they will spoil.

_____

_____

_____ 4. Dried legumes should never be soaked before cooking.

_____

_____

_____ 5. A sprout is a category used for a legume or grain that has started to germinate and sprout into a plant.

_____

_____

_____ 6. Grains are grasses that grow edible seeds.

_____

_____

_____ 7. The endosperm is the smallest part of the grain and provides a minor source of carbohydrates.

_____

_____

_____ 8. The pilaf method is a technique for cooking grains that includes sautéing the grain briefly in oil or butter, then simmering with stock or water and seasonings.

_____

_____

Part 3—Pasta

_____ 1. The word pasta comes from the Italian word for "paste", which refers to the flour, water, and egg mixture used to make pasta.

_____

_____

_____ 2. Dumplings are cooked balls of dough that include a filling and are found in many different cultures.

_____

_____

_____ 3. Carbo-loading is a method used by athletes that allows them to eat unlimited carbohydrates without affecting their weight.

_____

_____

_____ 4. Pasta cooked al dente is limp and easy to bite.

_____

_____

_____ 5. When making fresh pasta, the resting stage is the most important step in the process.

_____

_____

_____ 6. Spaetzle are small Italian dumplings, while gnocchi are small German dumplings made from bread.

_____

_____

_____ 7. When preparing the dough used for pasta or dumplings, it must always include a starch.

_____

_____

_____ 8. When working with pasta, it's important to match the sauce to the type of pasta.

_____

_____

Activity 11.2
Research/Demonstration—The Versatile Potato

Directions

Research the role of potatoes through history. You may be asked to research a specific culture or you can research potatoes in general. In your report, be sure to include the following information:

- What is a potato?

- When were potatoes introduced?

- How many potatoes does the average person consume?

- How are potatoes grown?

- Why are potatoes so important in many cultures?

- What are three unique potato recipes?

Take your notes in the space below. Present your findings to the class. Attach your recipes to this sheet.

_____

_____

_____

_____

_____

_____

_____

_____

_____

_____

_____

_____

_____

_____

_____

_____

_____

_____

Activity 11.3
Lab—Potato Cookery

Directions

Potatoes can be prepared in a variety of methods from baked to boiled, to deep-fried or served in a salad. They can be used as an entrée, a side dish, or a delicious snack. In this lab, you will experiment with several different uses of this versatile vegetable.

Recipe Selection

- Potato Lasagna with Wild Mushroom and Herb Sauce
- Roasted Potatoes with Garlic and Rosemary
- Glazed Sweet Potatoes
- Potato au Gratin

Objectives

After completing this lab activity, you should be able to:

- Apply effective *mise en place* through practice
- Demonstrate proper use of equipment and tools
- Follow basic food safety and sanitation guidelines
- Follow basic safety guidelines to avoid causing injury to self or others
- Match and cook potatoes to appropriate methods

Directions

1. Review the recipe you have been assigned.
2. Perform *mise en place*. Plan for any substitutions or additional instructions you have been given.
3. Prepare the recipe.
4. Clean up the area.

Potato Lasagna with Wild Mushrooms and Herb Sauce

Yield: 8 servings

Measure	Ingredients
8	Russet potatoes, sliced into ½-inch rectangles
12 oz	Butter, divided
6 oz	Shiitake mushrooms, sliced
6 oz	Oyster mushrooms, sliced
6 oz	Button mushrooms, sliced
6 oz	Chanterelle mushrooms, sliced
2	Shallots, chopped finely
12 oz	Beef or chicken stock
1 tbsp	Parsley, minced
2 oz	Roma tomatoes, diced

Directions

1. Place potato slices in single layer on a sheet pan brushed with 4 ounces butter. Bake at 350°F until tender.

2. Sauté mushrooms and shallots in 4 ounces butter. Cover and keep warm.

3. In saucepan, reduce stock by ¼. Add 4 ounces butter and blend.

4. Add parsley to stock and reserve warm.

5. To assemble each serving, place 1 potato slice at the bottom of a deep soup plate. Alternately layer mushroom mixture and 3 additional potato slices, finishing with potatoes. Drizzle sauce on each portion and garnish with diced tomatoes.

© Michael Zema, FMP/CCE. Used with permission.

Roasted Potatoes with Garlic and Rosemary

Yield: 10 servings

Measure	Ingredients
10	Red bliss potatoes, medium sized
1½ oz	Olive oil
1 tbsp	Garlic, crushed
1 tsp	Shallots, minced
1 tbsp	Fresh rosemary, chopped
To taste	Salt
To taste	Pepper

Directions

1. Scrub potatoes and dry thoroughly.

2. Combine oil, garlic, shallots, rosemary, salt, and pepper in a large stainless steel bowl. Add potatoes and toss to coat evenly.

3. Transfer potatoes to oiled pan and roast until tender, usually 20 to 25 minutes.

© **Michael Zema, FMP/CCE. Used with permission.**

Glazed Sweet Potatoes

Yield: 10 servings

Measure	Ingredients
3 lb	Sweet potatoes
8 oz	Fresh pineapple, cut into chunks
Juice from 1	Lemon
8 oz	Syrup
1 tsp	Cinnamon
2 oz	Butter

Directions

1. Bake sweet potatoes in a moderate oven at 350°F until tender. Cool.

2. Combine remaining ingredients in a saucepan and bring to a boil. Reduce to a simmer until mixture is thick.

3. Peel potatoes and cut into large chunks. Pour the glaze over the potatoes to coat.

4. Serve immediately.

© Michael Zema, FMP/CCE. Used with permission.

Potato Casserole

Yield: 10 servings

Measure	Ingredients
7 (about 3½ lb)	Chef's potatoes, large
16 fl oz	Heavy cream
8 fl oz	Milk
1 tsp	Garlic, minced
½ tsp	Salt
¼ tsp	Black pepper, freshly ground
3 tbsp	Butter, unsalted
5 oz (1¼ cups)	Cheddar cheese, grated

Directions

1. Peel the potatoes.

2. Slice them very thin (1/16-inch thick) by hand or on a mandolin. Reserve.

3. Combine the cream, milk, garlic, salt, and pepper.

4. Bring the mixture to a simmer.

5. Rub the butter in an even layer on the bottom and sides of a baking dish (10 x 12 inches).

6. Combine the potatoes and the cream mixture.

7. Place the mixture in the buttered pan.

8. Top with grated cheese.

9. Cover the pan with aluminum foil.

10. Bake the potatoes (in a hot-water bath, if desired) at 350°F until nearly tender, about 50 minutes.

11. Uncover and continue to bake until the potatoes are creamy and the cheese is golden brown, another 20 minutes.

12. Remove the potatoes from the oven and let them rest 10 to 15 minutes before slicing into portions.

13. Serve immediately or hold hot for service.

Activity 11.4
Matching—Legumes and Grains

Directions

Match the legume or grain to the correct descriptions.

	Cannellini/Italian Kidney	A.	Green, small, round
	Garbanzo/Chickpea	B.	Blue-black, tiny, round
	Mung	C.	Tan, buttery, kidney shaped
	Pigeon/Gandoles	D.	Nutty flavor, aromatic
	Bulgur	E.	Pure white, polished, soft wheat
	Hominy	F.	Dried kernels soaked in limewater
	Pearl	G.	Mildly nutty flavor, light brown, whole flour
	Pine/Pignoli	H.	Beige with orange spotting, small, heirloom
	Cake	I.	Mild flavor, off white, very tiny circles
	Masa	J.	Wide range of colors, sweet flavor
	Cashew	K.	Light brown, mild flavor, fine
	Groats	L.	White, nutty flavor, medium
	Basmati	M.	Tan to white, nutty flavor, variety
	Buckwheat	N.	Mild flavor, sticky, round, tiny
	Jasmine	O.	Black, red, or tan; crunch, sweet,
	Poppy	P.	Hulled, crushed grain
	Quinoa	Q.	Dried kernels soaked in lye
	Barley	R.	Light tan, buttery, small
	Sesame	S.	Brown or white, aromatic, nutty, extra long
	Amaranth	T.	Beige, acorn-shaped, nutty flavor

Activity 11.5
Lab—Cooking with Legumes

Directions

Legumes can be used in a variety of methods, from a cold salad to a refreshing entrée or a condiment used to enhance an entrée. There are also many cooking methods that can be used when working with legumes. As you have discovered, legumes can be prepared in many ways to enhance the flavor, texture, color, and nutrients.

Recipe Selection

- Bean Salsa
- Simple Split Pea Soup
- Refried Beans

Objectives

After completing this lab activity, you should be able to:

- Apply effective *mise en place* through practice
- Demonstrate proper use of equipment and tools
- Follow basic food safety and sanitation guidelines
- Follow basic safety guidelines to avoid causing injury to self or others
- Match and cook legumes to appropriate methods

Directions

1. Review the recipe you have been assigned.

2. Perform *mise en place.* Plan for any substitutions or additional instructions you have been given.

3. Prepare the recipe.

4. Clean up the area.

Bean Salsa

Yield: 16 oz

Measure	Ingredients
¾ cup	Fresh roasted corn kernels
16 oz	Cooked beans (use a variety for color and flavor)
½ cup	Red bell pepper, small dice
½ cup	Green bell pepper, small dice
⅓ cup	Red onion, small dice
1 tbsp	Fresh citrus juice
2 cloves	Roasted garlic, minced
1 small	Jalapeño pepper, seeded and minced
½ tbsp	Fresh oregano, minced
½ tbsp	Chili powder
½ tbsp	Ground cumin
1½ tbsp	Corn or other flavored oil
To taste	Kosher salt
To taste	Pepper

Directions

1. Combine all ingredients except oil, salt, and pepper.

2. Slowly add oil until desired consistency is reached.

3. Adjust seasoning with salt and pepper.

© Michael Zema, FMP/CCE. Used with permission.

Simple Split Pea Soup

Yield: 8 servings

Measure	Ingredients
2 cups	Onion, chopped medium
2 tsp	Vegetable oil
2 lbs	Split peas, dried
2 lbs	Ham bone
1½ lb	Ham, diced medium
10 cups	Water
To taste	Salt
To taste	Pepper

Directions

1. In a medium saucepan, sauté the onions in vegetable oil. Remove from heat.

2. In a stockpot, add the split peas, diced ham, ham bone, and sautéed onions.

3. Cover the mixture with water and cook over medium heat, stirring occasionally until the peas have broken down and become a thick green liquid. This will take approximately 2 hours.

4. You may need to add more water if the peas have not completely broken down. Check during the cooking process.

5. Add the salt and pepper.

6. Remove the soup from the heat and allow to set about 10 minutes so the soup thickens.

Note

For more flavor, simmer the ham bone in some water for 1 hour or more before making the soup to extract more flavor.

Variations

Other dried vegetables can be made into soups using a similar procedure. Most dried beans should be soaked in cold water overnight to reduce cooking time. (Split peas may be soaked, but they cook quickly enough without soaking).

Refried Beans

Yield: 9 servings

Measure	Ingredients
1 lb	Dried pinto or red beans
1 large	Onion, quartered
3 cloves	Garlic
½ tsp	Cumin, ground
3 drops	Hot pepper sauce

Directions

1. Cull, wash, and soak beans overnight.

2. Drain.

3. Place beans in a large saucepan and add water to cover by 2 inches.

4. Add onion and garlic.

5. Bring to a boil.

6. Cover and cook over low heat for 2 hours, or until the beans are very soft, adding water to keep the beans covered, if necessary.

7. Remove the onion and garlic, and discard.

8. Mash beans with a potato masher.

9. Season with cumin and hot pepper sauce.

10. Serve immediately, or hold hot for service.

Activity 11.6
Crossword Puzzle—Grains and Legumes

Directions

Complete the statements and answer the questions below. Use your answers to complete the crossword puzzle.

Across

7. The _____-_____ _____ is often served on New Year's Day to bring good luck.

11. The _____ seed is a tiny oval seed that can be used to make oil and tahini paste, or added to baked goods.

12. _____ is an aromatic rice with a delicate texture.

14. _____ is made from durum wheat and is used to make couscous and many types of pasta.

15. _____ is a tiny oval seed that can be eaten as cereal or made into oil.

16. The _____ bean is very popular in Japanese cuisine.

17. _____ is a type of corn used in succotash.

18. _____ is a type of grain used in paella and has a very high starch content.

Down

1. _____ is a type of corn used to make tortillas and other Mexican dishes.

2. The _____ is a small blue-black seed that is often used as a filling in baked goods.

3. The _____ is a brown nut that is served in both sweet and savory dishes.

4. The _____ is often served as an accompaniment or side dish.

5. The _____ is a kidney-shaped nut that is often used in baked goods.

6. _____ is a type of wheat used in tabbouleh.

8. _____ are seeds from pod-producing plants.

9. The _____ is often associated with being roasted over an open fire.

10. The _____ bean is the main ingredient in hummus.

13. _____ is a medium-grained wheat that is often served as an alternative to oatmeal.

15. The _____ bean is popular in many Mediterranean and Middle Eastern cultures.

www.CrosswordWeaver.com

Activity 11.7
Lab—Making Pasta from Scratch

Directions

Pasta in some form is found in almost every culture and can be found in many variations. In this lab, you'll be creating pasta from scratch. Try experimenting and enjoy!

Objectives

After completing this lab activity, you should be able to:

- Apply effective *mise en place* through practice

- Demonstrate the proper use of equipment and tools

- Follow basic food safety and sanitation guidelines

- Follow basic safety guidelines to avoid causing injury to self or others

Directions

1. Perform *mise en place*. Plan for any substitutions or additional instructions you have been given.

2. Prepare the pasta.

3. Clean up the area.

Basic Pasta Recipe

Yield: 2 servings

Measure	Ingredients
Approximately 1½ cups	All-purpose flour
2	Whole eggs, beaten
Pinch	Salt

Directions

1. Sift the flour into a large bowl (or in a mound on the prep table). Using your hands, make a well in the middle.

2. Beat the eggs and stir in the salt.

3. Pour the salt and egg mixture into the well you made in the flour.

4. Using your hands (or a fork), begin mixing the pasta. Use a circular motion and begin mixing from the center of the mixture. Keep mixing until the dough is firm, not squishy—you may need to add a little more flour in order to get the proper consistency.

5. Once the dough is mixed, use a clean area on the worktable and knead the dough for a short period of time. You will know it is ready when it has an elastic feel and a bit of a shine.

6. Roll the dough into a ball and wrap with plastic wrap. Set this aside for at least 15 minutes (although longer is better).

7. If you will be hand-rolling the dough, leave it aside for an hour or longer, and for ease of use, place in the refrigerator.

8. When you are ready to begin rolling the dough, divide the plastic-wrapped package into 2 balls.

9. Flatten the first piece into a rectangle and begin rolling. The second ball can remain in the refrigerator until ready to use.

10. After the dough has been rolled, run it through the pasta machine at the widest setting. Repeat this process 2 or 3 times.

11. Change the setting to a lower setting and run the pasta through again.

12. Repeat this process until the dough is the thickness you need.

13. When the dough is the correct thickness, cut the pasta.

14. Cook the pasta in a pot of salted, boiling water.

Activity 11.8
Lab—Cooking with Grains

Directions

Grains are an important staple food in many cultures. Even simple rice can be turned into flavorful, ethnic dishes when combined with the right ingredients and cooking methods. Now it's time to see these versatile grains in action.

Recipe Selection

- Chinese Fried Rice
- Polenta
- Rice Pilaf
- Risotto
- Spanish Rice

Objectives

After completing this lab activity, you should be able to:

- Apply effective *mise en place* through practice
- Demonstrate proper use of equipment and tools
- Follow basic food safety and sanitation guidelines
- Follow basic safety guidelines to avoid causing injury to self or others
- Use a variety of recipes and cooking techniques to prepare grains

Directions

1. Review the recipe you have been assigned.
2. Perform *mise en place*. Plan for any substitutions or additional instructions you have been given.
3. Prepare the recipe.
4. Clean up the area.

Chinese Fried Rice

Yield: 4 servings

Measure	Ingredients
6 slices	Bacon, minced
¾ cup	Onions, small dice
½ cup	Green bell peppers, small dice
½ cup	Celery, small dice
2½ cups	Cooked rice, cold
2	Eggs, slightly beaten
2 tbsp	Soy sauce
½ cup	Cooked small shrimp

Directions

1. Sauté bacon until slightly brown. Add onions, peppers, and celery. Sauté until all are al dente.

2. Add rice and sauté until slightly brown.

3. Add eggs, soy sauce, and shrimp.

4. Continue cooking for 5 to 7 minutes, adjusting seasoning with soy sauce.

© **Michael Zema, FMP/CCE. Used with permission.**

Polenta

Yield: Varies

Measure	Ingredients
5 pts	Stock or water
1 lb	Yellow cornmeal
2 oz	Oil, butter or other fat
To taste	Salt
To taste	Pepper

Directions

1. Mix all ingredients in a heavy stockpot. Heat mixture until thick.

2. Cover pot and transfer into a 350°F oven for 20 to 25 minutes.

3. Pour polenta into a greased pan, spreading mixture to desired thickness. Allow to cool.

4. After polenta has cooled, cut into desired shapes.

5. Polenta is now ready for pan-frying when needed.

Note

This is a basic recipe that can be modified with fresh herbs, Parmesan cheese, and/or sun-dried tomatoes.

© **Michael Zema, FMP/CCE. Used with permission.**

Rice Pilaf

Yield: 4 servings

Measure	Ingredients
½ oz	Oil, butter, or other fat
1 oz	Onions, small dice
1 cup	Long-grain white rice
2 cups	White stock
1	Bay leaf
To taste	Salt
To taste	Pepper

Directions

1. Heat oil, butter, or other fat. Add onions and sweat.

2. Add rice, and sauté for 3 to 5 minutes, making sure to coat well.

3. Add stock and bay leaf. Bring to boil, lower heat, and simmer for 15 to 20 minutes.

4. Remove bay leaf and adjust seasoning with salt and pepper.

Variations

Brown Rice Pilaf

Substitute brown rice for white rice. Add an additional ½ cup of stock and simmer for 45 minutes, following same cooking procedure.

Wild Rice Pilaf

Substitute wild rice for white rice. Add an additional ½ to 1 cup stock. Simmer for 45 minutes, following same cooking procedure.

For color and texture variety, add small diced bell peppers.

© Michael Zema, FMP/CCE. Used with permission.

Risotto

Yield: 6 servings

Measure	Ingredients
2 oz	Butter, divided
2 oz	Onions, brunoise
½ tbsp	Garlic, minced
6 oz	Arborio rice
2 oz	Chicken or veal stock
¼ tsp	Saffron threads, crushed
2 oz	Parmesan cheese, grated

Directions

1. Heat 1 ounce butter in a saucepan. Add onions and garlic, and sauté until translucent.

2. Add rice and toss to coat with butter. Do not let the rice brown.

3. Add a little stock to deglaze the pan; cook for 3 to 5 minutes.

4. Add remaining stock and saffron. Simmer until the stock has absorbed into the rice.

5. Add the cheese and remaining butter. Serve immediately.

Variations

Add various herbs with cheese and butter.

Substitute Asiago cheese for half of Parmesan cheese.

© **Michael Zema, FMP/CCE. Used with permission.**

Spanish Rice

Yield: 6 servings

Measure	Ingredients
2 tbsp	Olive oil
½ large	Green bell pepper, small dice
1 medium	Onion, julienne
1 clove	Garlic, minced
½ tsp	Dried basil
½ tsp	Dried rosemary
1 cup	Long grain white rice
1 cup	Tomatoes, concassé
½ tsp	Salt
⅛ tsp	Cayenne pepper
2 cups	White stock

Directions

1. Heat oil in a sauté pan. Add peppers, onion, and garlic, and sauté until al dente.

2. Stir in herbs, rice, tomatoes, salt, cayenne, and stock. Bring to boil over moderately high heat.

3. Cover, lower heat, and simmer for about 20 minutes or until rice is cooked.

© Michael Zema, FMP/CCE. Used with permission.

Activity 11.9
Menu Creation—Pasta Bar

Directions

You have been asked to design the menu for a new Italian restaurant opening in town. The restaurant will offer diners the opportunity to design their own pasta dishes by pairing noodles (pasta) and sauces. Create a menu listing at least eight pasta/sauce recommendations. If possible, create the menu on the computer. Be sure to include the following:

- Description of the noodle
- Description of the sauce
- Picture of the dish
- An interesting fact or suggestion

Take your notes in the space below. Present your menu to the class.

_____

_____

_____

_____

_____

_____

_____

_____

_____

_____

_____

_____

_____

_____

_____

_____

_____

_____

Activity 11.10
Poster/Presentation—Types of Pasta

Directions

Create a poster/presentation showcasing at least 12 different types of pastas. On your poster include the following information:

- Name
- Physical description
- Picture of the pasta
- Recommended cooking time
- An interesting fact about the pasta

This information can be displayed as a poster, electronic presentation, or some other type of visual. The pictures of the pasta can be images or actual pasta mounted on a board; whichever method is selected should be consistent for all pastas.

Take your notes in the space below. Share the presentation with your classmates, or invite another class in to view your presentation.

_____

_____

_____

_____

_____

_____

_____

_____

_____

_____

_____

_____

_____

_____

_____

_____

_____

Chapter **12**

Activity 12.1
Test Your Career Search IQ

Directions

Mark each of the following statements related to careers in the restaurant and foodservice industry as either true (T) or false (F). For each false statement, rewrite it to make it a true statement.

Part 1—Starting a Career in Foodservice

_____ 1. A career is a job that one takes to pay the bills.

_____

_____

_____ 2. A career ladder is a series of jobs through which people can advance to further their careers.

_____

_____

_____ 3. The only skills needed for a successful foodservice career are customer service skills.

_____

_____

_____ 4. One way to develop these skills now is to have a part-time job in the industry.

_____

_____

_____ 5. A mentor is someone who can play the role of an advisor and can offer insights into your career.

_____

_____

_____ 6. The best way to find a job is in the newspaper.

_____

_____

_____ 7. A résumé is a written summary of professional and educational experience.

_____

_____

_____ 8. A cover letter is used to capture the employer's attention so he or she will read your résumé.

_____

_____

Part 2—Completing Applications Effectively

_____ 1. The job application is important because it provides specialized information about the applicant.

_____

_____

_____ 2. When completing a job application, it is important to fill out every spot, even if it may not apply to you.

_____

_____

_____ 3. When applying for college or trade school, there are often strict deadlines that must be met.

_____

_____

_____ 4. A scholarship is a grant or financial aid given to a student to help him or her attend college.

_____

_____

_____ 5. It is not important to complete the FAFSA (Free Application for Federal Student Aid) if you do not want a scholarship.

_____

_____

_____ 6. The National Restaurant Association Educational Foundation (NRAEF) provides many scholarships for students interested in a career in the restaurant and foodservice industry.

_____

_____

Part 3—The Job Interview

_____ 1. During the job interview, the applicant and employer meet to discuss the applicant's qualifications for the position.

_____

_____

_____ 2. First impressions at the job interview do not matter.

_____

_____

_____ 3. It is always acceptable to appear for an interview wearing jeans and a t-shirt or flip-flops and shorts.

_____

_____

_____ 4. When meeting with a potential employer, it is important to use good manners throughout the meeting.

_____

_____

_____ 5. Depending on the job, it is not uncommon for an interview to last up to one hour.

_____

_____

_____ 6. Closed questions require detailed answers.

_____

_____

_____ 7. After the interview, the applicant should send a simple thank-you note.

_____

_____

_____ 8. Only non-U.S citizens are required to complete an I-9 form.

_____

_____

Activity 12.2
Building a Portfolio

Directions

Some employers may ask to see a portfolio of your work; other times, you may choose to bring a portfolio of your work with you to show an employer some of your skills that cannot translate well in a résumé. In this activity, you will be building a portfolio of your work from the past year. Your portfolio may have both an electronic presence or be paper only. Many employers will visit a personal Web site to see a portfolio.

Elements to include in the portfolio:

- Pictures of food created (garnishes, entrées, items that have unique presentations)
- Copies of exceptional class work, including:
  - Recipe books
  - Posters
  - Presentations or reports
- Certificate, awards, or other recognition
- Letters of recommendation

If you will be presenting a hard-copy portfolio, you will need a binder or presentation folder for copies of your work. If you are creating an electronic portfolio and your school does not provide access, you will need to create a Web site. There are several free sites available. A good site, with several templates related to education, is http://sites.google.com.

Create a list of the things that you plan to include in your portfolio in the space below.

_____

_____

_____

_____

_____

_____

_____

_____

_____

_____

Bonus activity: Prepare one of your favorite dishes as a live example of what you would take a picture of for your portfolio. If video equipment is available, have the demonstration filmed.

Activity 12.3
Research/Presentation—Career Opportunities

Directions

Research a career in the restaurant and foodservice industry that interests you and you can see yourself working in 10 to 15 years from now. Using resources such as the *Bureau of Labor Statistics Occupational Outlook Handbook*, career guides, and other resources, gather the following information and present it to your classmates. The presentation can be a poster, PowerPoint, or other electronic presentation or research paper. The following elements should be included:

- Name of position

- Job forecast for next 10+ years

- Average salary

- Education requirements

- Skills

- Typical career progression

- Potential job hazards

- Other interesting elements about the job

Take your notes in the space below. Present your findings to the class.

_____

_____

_____

_____

_____

_____

_____

_____

_____

_____

_____

_____

_____

_____

_____

_____

Activity 12.4
Practice Completing a Job Application

Directions

Name the foodservice job for which you are applying on the line below, and then complete the job application on the following two pages. Do not leave any areas blank. If something does not apply to you, write the letters "NA" (not applicable) in the space.

_____

Employment Application	Date

Personal Data (please print or type clearly)

Last Name:	First Name:	Middle Initial:
Street Address:	Telephone Number:	
City:	State:	Zip:

Are you legally eligible to work in the United States:	Yes	No
If hired, can you show proof of legal employment age?	Yes	No

Have you ever been convicted of a crime? If yes, please explain below.

How were you referred to this job?

Position applying for:

Applicable skills:

Educational Data

	Start Date	End Date
High School		
College/University		
Graduate School		
Trade/Business/Night Courses		
Other		

Employment Data

Employer	Dates: mm/yy to mm/yy	Starting Salary
		Ending Salary
Employer Address:		
City	State	Zip
Supervisor:	Supervisor's Title:	Phone:
Your Title:	Duties:	
Reason for Leaving:		

Employer	Dates: mm/yy to mm/yy	Starting Salary
		Ending Salary
Employer Address:		
City	State	Zip
Supervisor:	Supervisor's Title:	Phone:
Your Title:	Duties:	
Reason for Leaving:		

Do we have your permission to contact the above named employers for a reference?

_____ Yes   _____ No

Professional References (Please list only references that we may contact at this time)

Name	Title	Company	Phone

Agreement (please read the following statement carefully)

I hereby affirm that the information provided in this application (and accompanying materials, if any) is true and complete to the best of my knowledge. I acknowledge and agree that falsified information or significant omissions may disqualify me from further consideration for employment and may be considered justification for dismissal if discovered at a later date.

I authorize persons, schools, courts, current employer (if applicable), and previous employers and organizations named in this application (and accompanying materials, if any) to provide the organizations with any information that may be requested to arrive at an employment decision. I release all persons and entities and the organization from liability that may arise from such investigation and release of information.

I understand that neither this form, nor any organization documents, nor any statements made by the organizations constitutes an employment offer, contract, or obligation. Employment at the organization is "at will," and either the organization or I am free to terminate the employment relationship at any time, for any reason, with or without cause or notice.

Applicant's Signature and Date

Activity 12.5
Presentation—Choosing a College Program in Hotel/Restaurant Management or Culinary Arts

Directions

You will be researching trade schools and colleges that offer degrees and programs that will help you progress within the hospitality field. Create a presentation that allows you to compare different programs based on the following data:

- Location of school

- Degrees/programs offered

- Cost

- Size of school

- Accreditation (this may include regional and also professional)

- Graduate job placement rate

- Types of jobs graduates find after graduation

- Activities at the school

- Methods of class delivery (traditional, online, hybrid, weekend)

Use the information gathered to compare four different schools—if you have already decided what career you want to pursue, you may decide to research four schools that will help you reach this goal. If you haven't decided which career you want to pursue, consider researching four different types of schools, such as trade schools, community colleges, public universities, and private colleges. Use a variety of sources to gather your information, including guidance counselors, classroom teachers, the library, and the Internet, including the actual school Web sites.

Take your notes in the space below. Present your findings to the class.

_____

_____

_____

_____

_____

_____

_____

_____

_____

_____

_____

Activity 12.6
Financial Aid Options

Directions

Research scholarship opportunities for college students and also scholarship opportunities specifically geared for hospitality and culinary students. Develop a list of at least five but not more than ten scholarships that can be shared with the class. The following information should be included for each opportunity:

- Name of the scholarship (if applicable)

- Name of the sponsoring organization

- Link to information about the scholarship (Web address if applicable)

- Information about the scholarship:

  - Description of scholarship

  - Application deadline

  - Special requirements such as GPA, financial need, etc.

This material can be posted on a class Wiki or typed as a page to be submitted for a class reference book. Your instructor will provide details regarding the format.

Take your notes in the space below. Present your findings to the class.

_____

_____

_____

_____

_____

_____

_____

_____

_____

_____

_____

_____

_____

_____

_____

_____

Activity 12.7
Poster—Dress for Success

Directions

Review the material in your text that discusses how to dress for an interview. Create a poster or multimedia presentation showing a male and female student properly dressed for an interview and then showing what not to wear to an interview. Be sure to label or identify key elements for both aspects.

You can use pictures found online, in magazines, or even take pictures of your classmates dressed appropriately or inappropriately. Be creative.

Take your notes in the space below. Present your findings to the class.

_____

_____

_____

_____

_____

_____

_____

_____

_____

_____

_____

_____

_____

_____

_____

_____

_____

_____

_____

_____

_____

_____

Activity 12.8
Practice Interview

Directions

Today you are interviewing for a job at a local restaurant. You will be interviewed by one of the managers. The interview will last for approximately 7 to 10 minutes. (An actual interview may last for up to an hour, depending on the position.) Conduct yourself as if you were really applying for the position.

List of possible questions:

- Why do you want to work for this company?

- How did you hear about this position?

- Tell me about your last job.

- What skills do you have?

- What is your favorite class in school? Why?

- Tell me about a time when you had to solve a problem. What did you learn from the experience?

- How would you handle a customer complaint?

- Where do you see yourself in five years?

- If I were to ask your coworkers or classmates about you, what do you think they would tell me?

Note

You also may want to refer to the list of questions found in Chapter 12 in your text. Your interview may be recorded so you can see how you did. If the interview is recorded, use this as a learning tool.

After completing the interview, answer the following questions:

1. What did you learn about yourself?

_____

_____

_____

_____

_____

_____

2. What did you like least about the interview process?

_____

_____

_____

_____

_____

_____

_____

3. If you could change anything about the interview, what would it be and why?

_____

_____

_____

_____

_____

_____

_____

4. If your interview was recorded, did you notice anything about your presence that you would change?

_____

_____

_____

_____

_____

_____

_____

Activity 12.9
Create a Game Show—Health, Wellness, and Stress Management

Directions

You and your team have just been hired by the local television station to create a game show that will challenge viewers to test their knowledge of health, wellness, and stress management techniques. Your game show should be fun and interactive and should have two to three players or teams competing against each other. Each game should be based on a question/answer format similar to shows such as *Jeopardy!, Are You Smarter Than a Fifth Grader?,* or *Family Feud.* Each game should include the following:

- Not less than 25 but not more than 50 questions of varying levels of difficulty
- Instructions on how to play the game
- A game template or design for the questions to be presented
- Scoring rules
- A name for the game

Take your notes on how you plan to develop the game below. Present your game to the class.

_____

_____

_____

_____

_____

_____

_____

_____

_____

_____

_____

_____

_____

_____

_____

_____

_____

_____

Activity 12.10
Evaluating Blogs—Professional Development

Directions

You have been asked by the manager of a local restaurant to create a list of blog sites that can be used by the management team of the restaurant to stay current on the hot topics affecting the industry. Your task is to discover five blogs that address the following topics:

- Food safety

- Restaurant trends

- Job searching

- Marketing

- Health, wellness, and stress management

As part of your report to the manager you will need to create a report that answers the following questions about each site:

- The name of the blog

- The URL (Web address of the blog)

- Why you selected the blog

- Two facts that you learned from the blog

Each blog should be listed on a separate sheet of paper and then submitted as a booklet with a cover sheet. The cover sheet should include your name and the name of the project. You may choose to include a sample posting from each blog as part of your submission.

Take your notes in the space below. Present your findings to the class.

_____

_____

_____

_____

_____

_____

_____

_____

_____

_____

_____

_____